Edinbui .

Edinburgh Review
Editor: Alan Gillis
Assistant editor and production: Jennie Renton
Marketing and events: Lynsey May

Advisory Board: Janice Galloway, Kathleen Jamie, Robert Alan Jamieson,
James Loxley, Brian McCabe, Randall Stevenson, Alan Warner

Published by
Edinburgh Review
22a Buccleuch Place
Edinburgh EH8 9LN

edinburghreview@ed.ac.uk
www.edinburgh-review.com

Edinburgh Review 134: Neither Here Nor There
ISBN 978-0-9564983-5-9
ISSN 0267-6672

Edinburgh Review
is supported by

ALBA | CHRUTHACHAIL

Contents

Neither Here Nor There

Willy Maley

Tall Tales and Stilettos:
Muriel Spark's Short Stories[1]

When I told a colleague of mine I had read all twenty-two of Muriel Spark's novels he was surprised to learn there were so many and said smartly, 'They can't all be good.' They are. Another colleague, at a time when I had read only a handful of her short stories, said he thought Spark was actually a better short fiction writer than she was a novelist, which I felt could only be a backhanded compliment or a putdown. Having read all the stories I know different now. She is.

In a negative review of Muriel Spark's twentieth novel, *Reality and Dreams*, which appeared in the *New York Times* on 16 May 1997, Michiko Kakutani wrote:

> Here is the recipe for a typical Muriel Spark novel: take a self-enclosed community (of writers, schoolgirls, nuns, rich people, etc.) that is full of incestuous liaisons and fraternal intrigue; toss in a bombshell (like murder, suicide or betrayal) that will ricochet dangerously around this little world, and add some allusions to the supernatural to ground these melodramatics in an old-fashioned context of good and evil. Serve up with crisp, authoritative prose and present with 'a light and heartless hand'. [2]

Kakutani is perhaps a little light on the supernatural here, and a little hard on Spark, but she has the 'heartless hand' right, because Spark never wears hers on her sleeve as she has too many tricks up there already. Kakutani's most telling comment is her conclusion that 'As usual, Ms. Spark gives us no insight into the psychology of her characters or their motives'. This is telling because it's true; Spark has no interest in such psychologising, because her understanding of 'character' is far less shallow than that of Kakatuni and other like-minded critics.

Although 'famous for her poetry' at school, Muriel Spark's verse hasn't had the praise it may deserve, and her claim for her short stories – that they are the closest to poetry she gets in prose, unlike that 'lazy way of writing poetry'[3] called novels – has largely fallen on deaf ears. Interviewed in Paris in 1989, and asked about the difference between the short story and the novel, Spark answered:

> I feel the short story is superior, it's more difficult. If one is a perfectionist – it's not that I am exactly a perfectionist – but I like to get the very best out of every form. I really do think the short story is something by itself and it's superior to the novel in many ways. It's nearer to poetry and likely to have a longer life sometimes.[4]

In 1952 Spark published as part of her first collection of poems, *The Fanfarlo*, a poem entitled 'Evelyn Cavallo', a pseudonym she'd abandoned – 'This person never came to pass' – yet one who persists in rising from her 'fictitious grave', prompting the poet to ask exasperatedly:

> Why will you not lie down
>
> At the back of the neither here not there
> Where lightly I left you, Evelyn of guile?
> But no, you recur in the orgulous noonday style,
> Or else in your trite, your debonair
> Postprandial despair.[5]

I'll come back to 'orgulous' shortly. Spark's phrase, 'neither here not there', rather than 'neither here nor there', is a characteristic twist. Spark's notion of character is an odd one. In *Robinson*, January Marlow takes home impressions of faces to 'chew over it in privacy, as a wild beast prefers to devour its prey in concealment'.[6] In *Memento Mori*, in a long passage that is a flashback within a flashback, Alec Warner asks Jean Taylor unexpectedly whether 'other people exist? ... that people – the people around us – are real or illusory?'[7] In her short story 'Harper and Wilton' (1953), Spark's narrator is door-stepped by two fictional suffragettes bewailing their flimsily fatalistic depiction: 'Now you've got to give us substance otherwise we'll haunt you'.[8] The narrator is perplexed:

> Oh God, I remembered then that years ago, many, many years ago, some time in the 1950s, I wrote a story about two Edwardian suffragettes. What could I recall of that story? It was never published. Was it finished? I didn't find the two characters, Harper and Wilton, very sympathetic but I had certainly had some fun with them.[9]

In the original story, the narrator had the two suffragettes arrested for molesting a student – he had a squint so the cop couldn't tell which woman was the molester – but in the revised version at the urgings of her characters she has the tables turned, and 'in the light of the current correctness' it's the squint-eyed student who gets taken away, but only to be cautioned.[10]

The long story of Muriel Spark's short stories starts back in December 1951 when she won *The Observer* Christmas Short Story Prize with 'The Seraph and the Zambesi', selected from 6,700 entries, and ends – in one version – with the publication fifty years later, of *The Complete Stories*, forty-one tales all told. Her first collection, *The Go-Away Bird and Other Stories*, with eleven stories, appeared in 1958, the year after her debut novel. Thereafter there are six collections up to *All the Stories of Muriel Spark* (2001): *Voices at Play* (including radio plays, 1961); *Collected Stories I* (1967); *Bang-Bang You're Dead and Other Stories* (1983); *The Stories of Muriel Spark* (1985); and *Open to the Public: New and Collected Stories* (1997).

In 2003, two years after *The Complete Short Stories* appeared, there was another twist, when New Directions, a New York publisher with a long history of reissuing her work, released a volume entitled *The Ghost Stories of Muriel Spark*.[11] It comes with no introduction or explanation as to why these particular stories, and why this label? You may say she is an author who needs no introduction, that the stories stand alone, like that scarecrow 'Standing in the Field' (1994) in one of her poems, or 'That Lonely Shoe Lying on the Road' (1993) in another.[12]

Beautifully produced and presented, with a cover image by Man Ray – 'Fashion by Radio' (1934) – *The Ghost Stories of Muriel Spark* contains eight tales published over the previous fifty years, from 'The Seraph and the Zambesi' (1951), in which a real angel intervenes in a Nativity Masque, much to the distress of its organiser, before winging its way downriver 'among the rocks that look like crocodiles and the crocodiles that look like rocks', to 'The Hanging Judge' (1994), in which a magistrate, musing on the mechanics of strangulation, has an involuntary orgasm while passing sentence, then encounters a stiff of a colder kind sitting in the murderer's chair. There's a poem by Spark – 'The Victoria Falls' (1948) – that goes with 'The Seraph and the Zambesi'. (Her best stories all seem to have matching poems – 'The Go-Away Bird', the title tale of her first collection, published in 1958, started life as a poem she wrote while in Africa):

> Wrapped in this liquid turmoil who can say
> Which is the mighty echo, which the spray?[13]

These lines appear to echo Yeats's 'Among School Children': 'O body swayed to music, O brightening glance,/ How can we know the dancer from the dance?'

'The Seraph and the Zambesi' is interesting insofar as it predates Spark's 1954 conversion, and since she claimed her career as a novelist from 1957 was only made possible by her new-found faith – when of course it was kick-started by *The Observer* Short Story award – it's interesting that the supernatural and the religious are intertwined in that first story. Martin Stannard calls it 'arguably the first "postmodern", "magic-realist" text by a British author'.[14] But when the story appeared critics complained that it was '"an aimless trifle", and a "cheap skit"', or '"too artful"'.[15]

It's been said of Spark that 'her presentation of the supernatural does not conform to traditional religious definitions'.[16] In her 1953 study of John Masefield, Spark remarked 'how sharp and lucid fantasy can be when it is deliberately intagliated on the surface of realism'.[17] There are two new words, nice words, 'orgulous' from 'Evelyn Cavallo', meaning haughty – and 'intagliated' – carved or engraved – words that would sit well in a summary of Spark. Her stories are as orgulous and intagliated as all her work. 'God', said John Milton, 'every morning raines down new expressions into our hearts', and that's the only rain worth walking in.[18]

'The Seraph and the Zambesi' concerns the female narrator's encounter with a man called Samuel Cramer who turns out to be a refugee from a story by another writer, Charles Baudelaire, entitled 'La Fanfarlo' (1848). The narrator, visiting Victoria Falls for Christmas, has been sent to the gas station where Cramer rents rooms to tourists when there's no room at the inn. Cramer, as well as being a character cooked up by another author, and a petrol pump attendant, is also a writer. He has penned a Nativity play. This piece of amateur dramatics is interrupted by the appearance of a real Seraph, a celestial being who refuses to leave the stage. Cramer's native helpers throw petrol at the Seraph and the makeshift theatre burns down. They then chase the Seraph at seventy miles an hour till it disappears down the Zambesi, 'among the rocks that look like crocodiles and the crocodiles that look like rocks'. The story sees a confrontation between two typical Sparkean figures, creatures – or creations – deliberately designed to be unnatural or supernatural, the reincarnated literary character and the angel who threatens to mar his planned performance. Both are equally real, and equally unreal.

The supernatural in literature is a very large topic – and quite scary – but I want to touch on just a couple of perspectives.

The Supernatural From Trauma to Resistance

In an essay on James Joyce entitled 'The Ghosts of *Ulysses*', Maud Ellmann writes:

> Although most of us have grown embarrassed by racism, sexism, homophobia, and all the other violent exclusions which reveal the sacrificial logic of the modern state, we persevere in vivocentrism, the fiercest and perhaps the founding bigotry of all: the illusion that the living may eradicate the dead through burial, cremation, and forgetfulness. It is to protect the living from the dead that our culture insists upon their opposition, policing those extravagant and erring spirits who refuse to be confined to either realm.[19]

Ellmann cites Freud, from *Totem and Taboo* (1913), to the effect 'that ghosts are compromise formations which embody both reverence and horror towards the dead. He says that primitive societies first acknowledged death when they invented ghosts, yet this is also when they first denied it by asserting that the dead return'.[20] She also draws on Jacques Derrida's idea of writing as 'iterated anywhere, by anyone, independent of the life of its creator'.[21]

In a neglected text, a chapter from *Dialectics of Nature* on 'Natural Science in the Spirit World', dating from 1878, but dealing with the mediumistic craze and obsession with spirit photography of the 1840s, Friedrich Engels argued that the obsession with ghosts and the spirit world – helped along by the new technology of photography – was a retreat from politics, specifically from Chartism and the spectre of communism. Engels's deep disdain for the fakery of séances is shared by Spark in her novel *The Bachelors* (1960), but beyond such human-engineered trickery, Spark likes to unsettle her readers by weaving into her stories experiences and characters which are more ingenious spectres.

Modern writers have reacted differently to the politics of the ghost. Toni Morrison, by contrast to Engels, sees the supernatural not as a retreat from politics but as a site of resistance for excluded or marginalised or occulted communities. She says:

> [in *Song of Solomon*] I could blend the acceptance of the supernatural and a profound rootedness in the real world at the same time with neither taking precedence over the other. It is indicative of the cosmology, the way in which Black people look at the world. We are very practical people, very down-to-earth, even shrewd people. But within that practicality we also accepted what I suppose could be called superstition and magic, which is another way of knowing things. But to blend those two worlds together at the same time was enhancing, not limiting. And some of those things were 'discredited knowledge' that Black people had; discredited only because Black people were discredited therefore what they knew was 'discredited'. And also because the press toward upward social mobility would mean to get as far away from that kind of knowledge as possible. That kind of knowledge has a very strong place in my work.[22]

Morrison sees the relinquishing of the supernatural as linked with social mobility, where Engels identifies the class struggle and the censorship it endures as the cause of a turning towards spirit. Morrison's claim for the charged political nature of occulted communities and other ways of knowing can instructively be read against Engels's dismissal of the occult as a politics of retreat or defeatism. This is not to suggest that Spark is doing one or the other, retreating or resisting. She knew Africa – a little – and she knew the Scottish Gothic tradition too. She had her ancestral roots.

That idea of the supernatural as a retreat from politics or from trauma is something Spark touches on in her work when she reflects on the mediumistic craze of the 1940s and 1950s. During the war Spark worked as a spook in black propaganda, and this underpins her approach to the occult. In *A Far Cry from Kensington* (1988), set in the 1950s, Nancy Hawkins recalls:

> There was an upsurge of interest in the supernatural in those years, probably as a result of the uncontemplatable events which had blackened the previous decade.[23]

Where does Spark stand on the matter of creaky floorboards and hidden passages of history? She once remarked:

> I treat the supernatural as if it was part of natural history. If I write a ghost story it wouldn't come under the heading of ghost story necessarily because I treat it as if it was a natural thing.[24]

This natural approach to the supernatural was there before her conversion to Catholicism. It's the undercoat, as it were, over which goes the gloss. For Spark, religion was a question, not an answer:

> What I think about religion is that it would be preferable and more comfortable to have no religion in a sense, because then you know where you stand.[25]

Spark's sense of the supernatural as being bound up with religion is borne out by the earliest use of the word cited in the *Oxford English Dictionary*, from a religious treatise by William Bond, a Catholic cleric, dating from time of the Reformation, declaring that 'Fayth is a supernaturall lyght, & therfore it is indiuysyble, as all graces supernaturall be'.[26] On a similar note, Shakespeare, in *All's Well That Ends Well*, has Lafew comment caustically upon the premature pessimism around belief in the inexplicable, a disbelief in the miraculous that clearly has a Protestant inflexion:

> They say miracles are past; and we have our philosophical persons to make modern and familiar, things supernatural and causeless. Hence is it that we make trifles of terrors, ensconcing ourselves into seeming knowledge when we should submit ourselves to an unknown fear.[27]

Like Bond and Shakespeare, Spark saw no contradiction between faith and wonder. Asked whether she 'half' believed in ghosts 'or in an after-life' – as opposed to a half-life – Spark replied:

> Yes, I do. But not in the sense that one could possibly describe it. I have never seen a ghost. I have never had a real psychic experience that I felt a ghost in the room although I am sensitive to atmospheres, vibes as they call it. But I do think that this expresses something that can't be expressed, in any other form. The after-life exists but not in the form that you can say that the word 'after' or the word 'life' has any meaning. But it exists because we almost feel that it does in the way of what we've made of ourselves, the human race and its possibilities. Ghosts exist and we are haunted, whether we like it or not in the sense that it can only be expressed by a physical presence, or a ghost, but in fact, I do believe in the presence of something that you can call a ghost but not in the physical outline. I don't see any other way in which you can express this actuality, and I can't deny the actuality simply because there is no other way to express it.[28]

Thus ghostliness is for Spark bound up with faith and fiction in a way that makes her see things – as a writer and a convert – in ways distinct from the would-be rational reader. According to Robert Hosmer:

> Crucial and axiomatic to all Spark's fiction is an understanding that this world and the world beyond, the temporal and the spiritual, the quotidian and the transcendent, are inseparably integrated. No parallel reality theories ever captivated Spark. The natural and the supernatural are complementary, not contradictory.[29]

Reviews of Spark's stories usually begin by lamenting that the form is neglected, remarking the obsession with the supernatural, and praising the most 'realistic' ones. Of course, the short story itself is too blame, or criticism of it, but Spark's particular approach can appear as quaint, quick, quirky quackery to readers raised on realism. Spark herself put it like this:

> This border ballad savagery was what appealed to me, a much earlier state of being. Historically, I was very, very attracted to that.[30]

She added, 'I am very obsessional by nature.'[31] Asked about her 'fascination for the uncanny' Spark responded rather glibly: 'Oh yes. That's bound up with the border ballads and this Celtic twilight-feeling.'[32] But asked about the place of the uncanny in her work as 'a source of anguish', Spark replied in a more measured manner:

> There is a mutation … Things change but one goes on doing the same things for a different reason, the same activity. An original activity is very often based on all sorts of things, a sense of injustice, resentment, humiliation, all sorts of reasons why an artist becomes impelled to express himself.[33]

What gives rise to ghosts? Revenge? Injustice? The after-effects of trauma? A forced retreat into crawlspaces? The raising of the restless dead? All of the above?

In a poem entitled 'Authors' Ghosts' published shortly before her death, Muriel Spark mused

> I think that authors' ghosts creep back
> Nightly to haunt the sleeping shelves
> And find the books they wrote.[34]

If Spark returns to haunt her readers then those familiar only with *The Prime of Miss Jean Brodie* (1961) may get a fright, for in one of her guises – biographer, critic, editor, playwright, poet, novelist – this author wrote ghost stories. Indeed, on closer inspection, all her stories are ghost stories.

In 'The Executor', published in the *New Yorker* in 1983, Susan Kyle inherits her uncle's literary estate, but withholds one manuscript, an unfinished novel entitled *The Witch of the Pentlands*, whose author reaches back from beyond the grave to ensure the work is preserved according to his will. As a writer, the uncle is 'far out', meaning both weird and distanced:

> But far out was how he saw himself. He once said that if you could imagine modern literature as a painting, perhaps by Brueghel the Elder, the people and the action were in the foreground, full of colour, eating, stealing, copulating, laughing, courting each other, excreting, and stabbing each other, selling things, climbing trees. Then in the distance, at the far end of a vast plain, there he would be, a speck on the horizon, always receding and always there, and always a necessary and mysterious component of the picture; always there and never to be taken away, essential to the picture – a speck in the distance, which if you were to blow up the detail would simply be a vague figure, plodding on the other way.[35]

David Lodge found this tale 'rather trivial and mechanical in [the] use of the supernatural',[36] but Spark puts it up there with 'The Portobello Road' as among her best:

> 'The Portobello Road', I think, is my best. Or, maybe there was one which I wrote called 'The Executor', not long ago, which I think is up to the standard. What I think about the short story is that it leaves more also to the reader's imagination. Films are made of my books and stories. I don't make them. But if I were a director of a film, I would rather have a short story to work on than a novel because there is more field for imagination, more scope.[37]

Two of the most interesting stories in *The Ghost Stories of Muriel Spark* are 'The Girl I Left Behind Me' and 'The Portobello Road', featuring female murder victims telling their own tales, prototypes of Spark's own favourite novel – certainly her creepiest – *The Driver's Seat* (1970), a twist on Hitchcock's *Psycho*, the victim handpicking her own personal Norman Bates. The year she was starting out as a novelist, the year that her first novel, *The Comforters*, appeared, in which a woman called Caroline Rose found herself trapped in a book-world where a ghostly typewriter tapped out her thoughts, that year,

1957, three years after her conversion to Catholicism, after her breakdown, Spark published a strange little short story in *Ellery Queen's Mystery Magazine* entitled 'The Girl I Left Behind Me', its title based on an old marching song, from an old ballad – you can hear it in the 1950 John Wayne film *Rio Grande* – the girl in question, recovering from a long illness, works in an office for Mr Letter, who sits and hums while 'tie-gazing', freckled hands fretting at envelopes. She goes home one evening to her bedsit, 'anonymous among the homegoers', but feels she's forgotten something. What she finds on her return to work is not as gruesome as the joy it gives her:

> A clock struck quarter past seven as I got off the bus. I realized that again I had not paid my fare. I looked at the money in my hand for a stupid second. Then I felt reckless. 'Teedle-um-tum-tum' – I caught myself humming the tune as I walked quickly up the sad side street to our office. My heart knocked at my throat, for I was eager. Softly, softly, I said to myself as I turned the key of the outside door. Quickly, quickly, I ran up the stairs. Only outside the office door I halted, and while I found its key on my bunch it occurred to me how strangely my sister would think I was behaving.
>
> I opened the door and my sadness left me at once. With a great joy I recognized what it was I had left behind me, my body lying strangled on the floor. I ran towards my body and embraced it like a lover.[38]

In the following year, 1958, Spark published 'The Portobello Road', in the Italian magazine *Botteghe oscure*, in which a girl nicknamed Needle after pricking her thumb on one in a haystack is confided in by a male acquaintance, who plans to marry despite having a wife back in Africa. When Needle threatens to tell the truth, the man is raging:

> He looked as if he would murder me and he did. He stuffed hay into my mouth until it could hold no more, kneeling on my body to keep it still, holding both my wrists tight in his huge left hand. I saw the red full lines of his mouth and the white slit of his teeth last thing on earth. Not another soul passed by as he pressed my body into the stack, as he made a deep nest for me, tearing up the hay to make a groove the length of my corpse, and finally pulling the warm dry stuff in a mound over this concealment, so natural-looking in a broken haystack.[39]

The headline, '"Needle" is found: in haystack!' is one of a series of odd moments that follow the murder scene, ending in Needle confronting her killer on Portobello Road 'nearly five years later'. The story contains a passage early on which is close to the 'far out' storytelling uncle in 'The Executor', where the ghostly Needle, browsing in the Portobello Road market, alludes to herself wandering:

> most Saturdays … among the solemn crowds with their aimless purposes, their eternal life not far away, who push past the counters and stalls, who handle, buy, steal, touch, desire and ogle the merchandise. I hear the tinkling tills, I hear the jangle of loose change and tongues and children wanting to hold and have.[40]

In 'the jangle of loose change and tongues' picked up by a ghost we see Spark's lucid use of the supernatural. 'The Portobello Road' has always been singled out as 'up to the standard', and was reprinted in *The Norton Book of Ghost Stories* in 1994.[41]

In her biography of Mary Shelley, Spark rejected the term Gothic as too vague, preferring to see *Frankenstein* as 'a new and hybrid fictional species'. Spark, like Shelley, wedded the bizarre and the businesslike, the supernatural and scientific, making what she says of Shelley sound like self-reflection:

> The horror produced by Gothicism was dissipated in vapour, but Frankenstein's sharp outlines intensified the horror element to a most sinister degree.[42]

We've heard of ghost writers and ghost characters, but what if all literary characters are ghosts and what if that ghostliness extends to – heaven forfend – real characters, including authors? In *Memento Mori*, in the Maud Long Medical Ward, there's a conversation between Jean Taylor and Alec Warner that leads Jean into a double-embedded memory in which Alec asked, unexpectedly:

> 'Do you think, Jean, that other people exist? … that people – the people around us – are real or illusory?' …
>
> 'This graveyard is a kind of evidence, that other people exist … But the graves are at least reassuring,' she said, 'for why bother to bury people

if they don't exist?'

    'Yes, oh precisely,' he said.[43]

Precisely. And there's the rub. Headstones and hallucinations are the evidence of the graveyard. The greatest trick the Devil – or the Dame – ever pulled was convincing characters – and readers – they really exist. Because of course, neither Alec nor Jean are 'real people' – merely characters in a novel, ciphers (or 'cybers') in a book, entranced carcasses.[44] Spark questions the basis of character, in and out of books. Here, in a couple of pages, she sketches a lifelong relationship, then erases it.

Short Shrift From Reviewers

Early reviewers of Spark's short stories were often unsure how to respond, or they were just plain hostile. Take Benjamin De Mott, who reads like a character from Spark's fiction. In a demotic review essay entitled 'In and Out of Storytown', published in the *Hudson Review* in 1961,[45] De Mott began by stating the obvious, namely that short stories get a bad press, then added that this was not merely a matter of prejudice, but because the form exposes writers who are merely competent:

> Competence in long forms increases a reader's respect for the major achievements of literary art; in short forms it brings to mind the aesthetic of Disneyland, which sees the imagination as a racket operated for kids.[46]

De Mott detects in Spark a 'contempt for cant' that trumps 'the love of truth'.[47] Spark, says De Mott, 'begins with the cant, not with the person.'[48] That seems fair enough – though since when was a character a person? – except it's not what De Mott wants. He wants blood. Of 'Daisy Overend' and 'The Black Madonna' he says 'the pattern of both tales is once again the formulaic dirt-doing on sentimentality … It is ever thus in Storytown: idealism shown its corruption, stick figures beaten with sticks.'[49] De Mott, like other negative reviewers, sees the title tale of *The Go-Away Bird* as its redeeming feature:

> There are other devices in *The Go-Away Bird* that operate only a shade less

mechanically than Mrs. Spark's reducing machine for liberals, and that are readily seen as the inventions of the same rapid, clever, cynical mind which shines like a lucid loin in *Memento Mori* and *The Ballad of Peckham Rye* – the novels that have lately strengthened this writer's American reputation. Sci-Fi and supernaturalism figure in 'The Portobello Road,' 'The Seraph and the Zambesi,' and 'Miss Pinkerton's Apocalypse' – pieces about reincarnation, flying saucers, talking corpses and other subjects of interest to the audience of *Punch* (that magazine has in fact printed Mrs. Spark) or of Roald Dahl. But the title piece of the collection is fiction at an altogether different level … it redeems this collection and stands as Mrs. Spark's most considerable achievement to date.[50]

Here, the weight of Spark's deftness of touch is both felt – she has clearly got her nails deep into De Mott – and at the same time dismissed – she is merely light-fingered, and lacking in substance.

Another example. Reviewing Spark's *Collected Poems I* and *Collected Stories I* together with her latest novel *The Public Image* in 1968, Christopher Ricks was quite scathing, taking issue not just with Spark but her apparent protectors:

Mrs. Spark's poems are pastiche. Sometimes skilled. But skill glitters from all her fiction – from her new novel, *The Public Image*, as from her *Collected Stories: 1*. Does it do more than glitter?

…

'I have forgotten her name but I shall remember it at the Bar of Judgment.' So ends a story which indicts ('diminutive, charming, vicious') a woman whose name till the Day of Judgment is going to have to be Daisy Overend. Most of the stories and novels set up a Bar of Judgment. Yet what is odd, to the point of being artistically suicidal, is their guilt before their own tribunal. They exemplify more than any other writing known to me, a body of work guilty of all that which it finds most hateful and which it most eagerly exposes. Mrs. Spark is the great example of the novelist as ferret, and yet what her novels most deplore is the ferret … Yeats believed that literature was 'the Forgiveness of Sin,' and even those who don't agree with him about that may still see what he means when he rejects the idea of literature as accusation: 'when we find it becoming the

Accusation of Sin, as in George Eliot, who plucks her Tito in pieces with as much assurance as if he had been clockwork, literature has begun to change into something else.' Mrs. Spark plucks all her characters in pieces as if they had been clockwork.[51]

Certainly in 'The Ormolu Clock' and in the children's story, *The Very Fine Clock*, published in the same year as Ricks' review, but not included as part of her collected or later complete stories, Spark can be seen to be taking characters apart, as she has January Marlow do in *Robinson* (1958). It's not for the faint-hearted, but nor is it for those who believe in the truth of character. In other words, it's not for the delusional or the demoniacally possessed.

Richard Johnson, in a 1972 review of the same collection, takes issue with Ricks, while acknowledging that his is a view that cannot be ignored (much as we would like to).[52] Johnson enlists Aristotle in order to suggest that in the best tradition of tragedy Spark is more preoccupied with action than character.[53] Johnson concludes:

> This, I think, is a proper gloss to Mrs. Spark's fictions: she does not attempt directly to represent character, but rather to make plots that imitate actions. She is a maker of plots that show us character acting; she does not try to create fiction that we are looking at 'real' characters in depth. And I think she is not a lesser artist for adopting this approach. Starting with what may well seem 'cardboard' characters by the standards of Victorian fiction and treating them with stylistic acerbity, Mrs. Spark makes tales that, without resorting to extravagance of language or detail, create a sense – though never an explanation – of the density and complexity of life and lives.[54]

Tom Hubbard, in his 1984 essay on Spark's short stories, also defends her use of the supernatural:

> Muriel Spark is not an escapist. Her work cannot be dismissed on the grounds of irresponsible frivolity or pseudo-mysticism. She believes in a dimension beyond the human, yet that impels her not to deny human life but to criticize it.[55]

Adam Thirlwell, in one of the most lucid and engaging analyses of Spark I have read, appears to 'get her', and to have the measure of Ricks:

> This deadpan lack of explanation or emotion can scare some critics. It has scared Christopher Ricks. In an essay in the *New York Review of Books*, in 1968, Christopher Ricks made the case against Muriel Spark as cruelly seeking to expose her characters' frailties: 'human beings cannot but be opaque … so ought our artistic ideal be, above all, to see through them?'
>
> In her great novel *Memento Mori*, Spark offers this conversation, in a nursing home – an implicit anticipatory rebuke to critics like Ricks.
>
> > 'And yet,' said Charmian, smiling up at the sky through the window, 'when I was half-way through writing a novel I always got into a muddle and didn't know where it was leading me.' Guy thought: She is going to say – dear Charmian – she is going to say 'The characters seemed to take on a life of their own.' 'The characters,' said Charmian, 'seemed to take on a life of their own.'
>
> It is a form of literary sentimentality to believe, as Ricks does, that a character can be opaque to his or her author – though, in one crucial respect, Spark's characters are opaque. When they behave evilly, they behave out of character. Their psychology, psychology in general, will not help us understand them. But this is not the opacity Ricks means.
>
> The reason for Muriel Spark's concision is this – character is much less complicated than we like to think. Everyone is so much simpler.[56]

I follow Thirlwell up to a point, but the idea of character for Spark isn't that it's simple, or that characters behaving badly are acting 'out of character'. No, for Spark, character is not just an invention, a fiction, it's a front and even an affront to God. Possession is nine-tenths of character – the rest is cardboard or corrugated irony.

Contrary to Thirlwell's otherwise penetrating critique of Ricks, Spark really did believe in evil as well as ghosts. In an interview in 2001 with John Tusa, Spark said:

> I really do think that the devil exists. I think evil exists. I think we see it everywhere.[57]

In an early poem entitled 'Against the Transcendentalists' (1952) Spark wrote:

> Who is Everyman, what is he
> That he should stand in lieu of
> A poem? What is the truth of it?
> And what good's a God's-eye view of
> Anyone to anyone
> But God? In the Abstraction
> Many angels make sweet moan
> But never write a stanza down.
> Poets are few and they are better
> Equipped to love and animate the letter.[58]

Interestingly, speaking of her biggest – and in my view her best – book, *The Mandelbaum Gate* (1965), a book that critics thought was too big for its boots, too political for a lady with a light touch, Spark said:

> I took a long time to do that book, I took two years. After writing two books a year, one book in two years was a long time. It's a long book. I did it in the form of short stories; each chapter was a short story with a different point of view. They published most of it in the *New Yorker*. How did I feel afterwards? I was very exhausted. I was not sure that I wanted to do anything more like that; I felt I had done my *Passage to India*. I felt I'd got out of myself what I wanted to say, but I certainly didn't want to go in for more sociological books.[59]

It's strange to hear Spark describing this seething and substantial book as a collection of short stories, but it reminds us that book chapters, novel chapters, are also often short stories in their own right, often even separately published as such.

Spark's writing practice entails a kind of private communing: 'I talk to myself; it's a dialogue with myself largely'.[60] Asked whether she was a modernist writer Spark suggested she was postmodernist, or at least that's what some critics thought. Asked what that meant, she replied:

> Well I think that it means that there is another dimension which is a bit

creepy, supernatural ... not supernatural but not necessarily, consequential. I always think that causality is not chronology. I go on that; one thing doesn't necessarily lead to another inevitable thing, although it does lead to something else in actual fact.[61]

Spark's subtly surreal style was arguably enhanced by her experiences as a starving artist under the influence of Dexedrine, which she took as an appetite suppressant in 1954. It was, she said, 'a mad idea', out of which came mad ideas. She was also under the influence, when it came to short stories, of Guy de Maupassant, Henry James, Mary Lavin, Edgar Allan Poe, Wilkie Collins, Jorge Luis Borges.

Most of the stories in *The Complete Short Stories* (2001) could qualify as ghost stories. 'The Twins' (1954) echoes Henry James's *Turn of the Screw*; 'Miss Pinkerton's Apocalypse' (1955) reads like a pilot for *The League of Gentlemen*, in which a flying saucer – of the crockery variety but with radioactive properties – wings through the window while local shopkeeper Laura Pinkerton is 'doing something innocent to the fire'; in 'The Pearly Shadow' (1955) a psychiatric patient sees a translucent apparition, and since this is a Spark story, so does his psychiatrist; the ghastly 'Quest for Lavishes Ghast' (1964) takes a haunting phrase too far; 'The Playhouse Called Remarkable' (1967) is a misbegotten sci-fi story on the Changing Drama of the Moon; 'The First Year of my Life' (1975) is told by a telepathic toddler, a midnight child with a nice line in sarcasm (always first and fastest, Spark got there before Salman Rushdie or Irvine Welsh); 'The Dragon' (1985) has shades of Alasdair Gray about it, Spark's 'dragon-stitch' a needlepoint version of Lanark's 'Dragonhide'; 'Going Up and Coming Down' shows you don't have to be a member of the Cosmic Paranormal Apostolic Movement to meet your match in an elevator, but it helps; 'Christmas Fugue' (2000) reprises the coastal fever of *The Mandelbaum Gate*, as a passenger on a long-haul flight fancies she makes love to the pilot only to realise her fly fug was a fantasy; and 'The Young Man Who Discovered the Secret of Life' (2000) is 'haunted by a ghost about five feet high when unfurled and standing upright'.

In 'The Dragon' (1985), 'The essence of the dragon-stitch is that you see all the stitches'.[62] But nobody said seeing the stitches made the monster any less scary. In 'The Dark Glasses' (1961), 'psychic manifestations of sex' and child poltergeists are the least of our worries, because seeing is bad enough:

'These fishers of the mind have no eye for outward things'.[63] The novelists of consciousness miss the ghostwriting on the wall that says the spirit in the human machine is a story made up to ward off the wolf.

'The Gentile Jewesses' (1963), like most of Spark's stories, is about faith and fiction. When the narrator's mother bows to the moon, as Spark's mother did, and as January Marlow does in *Robinson*, she shows there's room in her cosmology for the moon and the Madonna. Spark never ran away, never hid, from nature or the supernatural. In *Curriculum Vitae* she recalls:

> My mother was full of superstitions and presentiments. She wouldn't wear green. But I knew that this was mad from the evidence of perfectly happy people I saw wearing green. Her terror of thunder and lightning likewise had no effect on me. She would huddle with me into a darkened room during a thunderstorm, but as soon as I got away on holiday to the seaside at Crail in Fife, I ran down to the wonderful beach to watch thunderstorms in progress over the North Sea.[64]

The couple at the end of *The Takeover* (1976) sit staring at 'the bashed-in circle of the moon' because that's the only coin in the fountain of the firmament. But there's always a twist. Another Spark gem, 'The Black Madonna' (1958), a brilliant indictment of racist hypocrisy, appeared in Carl MacDougall's 1989 anthology *The Devil and the Giro* (1989). In his introduction, MacDougall observed:

> Our fascination with the supernatural is not as simple as it might seem and Scottish writers have seldom opted for straightforward ghost stories or tales of the unexpected.[65]

Spark's critique of realism doubles as anti-authoritarianism, deconstructing the concept of individual consciousness on which such authoritarianism depends, and with it the rule of capitalism. That's why she's more radical than all the individualists and existentialists put together. Personality disorder and character assassination mean little to Spark. Personality is disorder, character is assassination, forms of 'possession' conjured up by capitalism to serve its own interests. Death to character! There's an expression where I come from – perhaps it's widely known – of giving someone their character, meaning taking them down a notch or two, telling home truths. Spark gives characters their character and in the process gives her naturally supernatural readers – possessed by possessive individualism – theirs too.

But what's the relationship between a character and a person? Do they both have authors? Shakespeare's Coriolanus declares:

> … I'll never
> Be such a gosling to obey instinct, but stand
> As if a man were author of himself
> And knew no other kin.[66]

The self is a con trick, a sleeve-tuck that hides the truth. Spark is a trickster, a pearly shadow. Exorcisms, ventriloquism, sleights of hand are her box of tricks, her medium. David Lodge, in a fuller review, wrote:

> The writings of Muriel Spark illustrate very clearly the idea, put forward by the Russian Formalists earlier in this century, that the function of art is 'to defamiliarise or make strange' the world, to overcome the deadening effects of habit on our perceptions.[67]

Lodge sees Spark's stories, especially 'The First Year of My Life', in which a baby reports on the First World War from the vantage point of the cradle, as designed to defamiliarise, to make strange:

> The premise of the story is … a kind of electronic updating of the neo-platonic idea, memorably formulated in Wordsworth's 'Intimations of Immortality' ode, that we are born with supernatural powers of perception that quickly atrophy in mundane existence.[68]

But this story, it transpires, is as good as it gets, for Lodge goes on to say:

> There is perhaps nothing else quite as stunningly original in this volume as 'The First Year of My Life,' and some of the contents fall very far below it in quality. Indeed, as a 'collected stories,' the book is slightly disappointing. To put this judgment in perspective, I should say that I consider Mrs. Spark to be the most gifted and innovative British novelist

of her generation, one of the very few who can claim to have extended and altered the possibilities of the form for other practitioners. If she does not consistently impress one as being a short-story writer of the same calibre, it may be because the bold economy of her novelistic technique sometimes seems like a cutting of corners in the more confined space of the short story …

Many of the stories turn on events that are supernatural or preternatural, and several are ghost stories. If we adopt the French critic Tzvetan Todorov's distinction between 'the fantastic' – in which there is always a possible naturalistic explanation of the uncanny; and 'the marvellous' – in which there is not – it is clear that Mrs. Spark's fiction usually falls into the second category. This is consistent with her uncompromising, if idiosyncratic, Roman Catholic faith. Ghosts, miracles, visitations by angels and demons have figured prominently in her work … The use of the supernatural in fiction, especially in the mode of the 'marvelous' rather than the 'fantastic,' is always a risky proceeding because it can seem too easy a way of transfiguring the commonplace.[69]

Of 'The Black Madonna' Lodge says:

In this story there is a streak of that authorial vindictiveness toward her own characters which some readers cite as a reason for not succumbing to Mrs. Spark's literary skill. It is perfectly true that her imagination is fascinated by revenge, humiliation and ironic reversals, and that she looks upon pain and death with a dry, glittering eye. Nevertheless, in the novels, if not always in the short stories, this cruel streak in her work is restrained and tempered by the comic spirit.[70]

The novels, for some critics, redeem themselves with 'divine comedy', and by diluting the occult element.

Dean Flower, reviewing Spark's *Open to the Public: New and Collected Stories* (New Directions, 1998), remarked:

The fascination of Spark's storytelling lies in what she gets away with. She has been able to violate almost any rule of fiction. Her narrators range from ghosts to newborn infants. She never writes about herself and yet almost always uses the first person. Just when you expect devastating irony, something odder and more authentic occurs. If death is on the telephone or an angel must be dealt with, Spark makes it seem perfectly normal.[71]

Spark gets away with a lot, and yet she lets readers away with nothing. She demands all our attention, and she demands that we take her seriously, even when we think she's being plain mischievous, telling tall tales with a twist for the sake of being twisted, rather than making a telling point. It was Stuart Kelly who said: 'Spark uses a stiletto; McIlvanney uses a broadsword.'[72] You can arguably say more with a claymore, but the point will always be taken and driven home more emphatically and to greater effect with a stiletto.

Endnotes

1. This essay is the text of the Annual Muriel Spark Lecture delivered at the National Library of Scotland on 16 November 2011. I am grateful to the Muriel Spark Society for extending the invitation to speak, and in particular to Gail Wylie and Eric Dickson.

2. 'Her Serene Tyranny, A Mistress of Mayhem', *New York Times* (16 May, 1997), p. 29.

3. Alan Bold, *Muriel Spark*, Contemporary Writers (London: Methuen, 1986), p. 30.

4. Jeanne Devoize and Pamela Valette, 'Interview with Muriel Spark', *Journal of the Short Story in English* 41 (2003), http://jsse.revues.org/index328.html. Accessed 09 November 2011.

5. Muriel Spark, *All the Poems* (Manchester: Carcanet, 2004; 2006), p. 66.

6. Muriel Spark, *Robinson* (London: Macmillan, 1958; New York: New Directions Classic, 2003), p. 137.

7. Muriel Spark, *Memento Mori* (London: Macmillan, 1959; Harmondsworth: Penguin, 1973), pp. 67-69.

8. Muriel Spark, 'Harper and Wilton', *The Complete Short Stories* (London: Penguin, 2001), p. 193.

9. Spark, 'Harper and Wilton', p. 193.

10. Spark, 'Harper and Wilton', p. 197.

11. Muriel Spark, *The Ghost Stories of Muriel Spark* (New York: New Directions, 2003).

12. Spark, *All the Poems*, p. 50, p. 52.

13. Spark, *All the Poems*, p. 53.

14. Martin Stannard, 'Nativities: Muriel Spark, Baudelaire, and the Quest for Religious Faith', *The Review of English Studies* 55, 218 (2004), p. 91.

15. Stannard, 'Nativities: Muriel Spark, Baudelaire, and the Quest for Religious Faith', p. 94.

16. Ann B. Dobie, 'Muriel Spark's Definition of Reality', *Critique* 12, 1 (1970), p. 23.

17. Muriel Spark, *John Masefield* (London: Peter Nevill, 1953; revised edition, London: Pimlico, 1992), p. 165, cited in Tom Hubbard, 'The Liberated Instant: Muriel Spark and the Short Story', in Alan Bold (ed.), *Muriel Spark: An Odd Capacity for Vision* (London: Vision and Barnes & Noble, 1984), p. 169.

18. Milton, *Eikonoklastes* (1649), in Don Wolfe (ed.), *Complete Prose Works of John Milton* (Nw Haven: Yale University Press, 1962) 3: 506-7.

19. Maud Ellmann, 'The Ghosts of *Ulysses*', in Augustine Martin (ed.), *James Joyce: The Artist and the Labyrinth: A Critical Evaluation* (Ryan Publishing: London, 1990), p. 194.

20. Ellmann, 'The Ghosts of *Ulysses*', p. 197. See Freud, *Totem and Taboo*, pp. 65-66.

21. Ellmann, 'The Ghosts of *Ulysses*', p. 197.

22. Toni Morrison, 'Rootedness: The Ancestor as Foundation', in Dennis Walder (ed.), *Literature in the Modern World: Critical Essays and Documents* (Oxford: Oxford University Press, 1990), p. 330.

23. Muriel Spark, *A Far Cry from Kensington* (London: Constable and Company, 1988; Harmondsworth: Penguin, 1989), pp. 103-104.

24. James Brooker and Margarita Estévez Saá, 'Interview with Dame Muriel Spark', *Women's Studies* 33, 8 (2004), p. 1036.

25. Brooker and Saá, 'Interview with Dame Muriel Spark', p. 1037.

26. William Bond, *Pilgrimage of Perfection* (1531; first published in 1526), iii, f. Clxxxx.

27. William Shakespeare, *All's Well That Ends Well*, 2.3.1-6, ed. G. K. Hunter, in *The Arden Shakespeare Complete Works*, gen. eds. Richard Proudfoot, Ann Thompson and David Scott Kastan (London: Thomson Learning, 2007), p. 99.

28. Devoize and Valette , 'Interview with Muriel Spark'.

29. Hosmer, 'The Short Stories of Muriel Spark', p. 457.

30. Devoize and Valette , 'Interview with Muriel Spark'.

31. Devoize and Valette , 'Interview with Muriel Spark'.

32. Devoize and Valette , 'Interview with Muriel Spark'.

33. Devoize and Valette , 'Interview with Muriel Spark'.

34. Spark, *All the Poems*, p. 13.

35. Spark, *The Ghost Stories of Muriel Spark*, pp. 82-83.

36. David Lodge, 'Marvels and Nasty Surprises', *New York Times* (October 20, 1985), http://www.nytimes.com/1985/10/20/books/marvels-and-nasty-surprises.html, accessed 13 November 2011.

37. Devoize and Valette , 'Interview with Muriel Spark'.

38. Muriel Spark, 'The Girl I Left Behind Me', *The Complete Short Stories*, pp. 222-223.

39. Spark, 'The Portobello Road', *The Complete Short Stories*, p. 412.

40. Spark, 'The Portobello Road', *The Complete Short Stories*, p. 396.

41. Muriel Spark, 'The Portobello Road', in Brad Leithauser (ed.), *The Norton Book Of Ghost Stories* (New York: W. W. Norton and Company, 1994), pp. 318-336.

42. Muriel Spark, *Child of Light: A Reassessment of Mary Wollstonecraft Shelley* (Hadleigh: Tower Bridge Publications, 1951); revised as *Mary Shelley* (London: Constable, 1988; 1993), p. 171.

43. Spark, *Memento Mori*, pp. 67-71.

44. I'm thinking here of the moment in Spark's first novel when one character listens to her grandson, Laurence Manders, a sports commentator with the BBC: 'Louisa Jepp sat beside the wireless cuddled in the entranced carcass of Laurence's voice'. *The Comforters* (London: Macmillan, 1957; Harmondsworth: Penguin, 1963), p. 172.

45. Benjamin De Mott, 'In and Out of Storytown', *The Hudson Review* 14, 1 (1961), pp. 133-141.

46. De Mott, 'In and Out of Storytown', p. 133.

47. De Mott, 'In and Out of Storytown', p. 136.

48. De Mott, 'In and Out of Storytown', p. 137.

49. De Mott, 'In and Out of Storytown', p. 137.

50. De Mott, 'In and Out of Storytown', p. 138.

51. Christopher Ricks, 'Extreme Instances', *The New York Review of Books* (19 December 1968): 31–32, http://www.nybooks.com/articles/archives/1968/dec/19/extreme-instances/, accessed 13 November 2011.

52. Richard A. Johnson, 'Review of Muriel Spark, *Collected Stories: I*', *Studies in Short Fiction* 9, 3 (1972), pp. 289-291, esp. p. 290.

53. Johnson, 'Review of Muriel Spark, *Collected Stories: I*', p. 290.

54. Johnson, 'Review of Muriel Spark, *Collected Stories: I*', pp. 290-291

55. Tom Hubbard, 'The Liberated Instant', p. 178.

56. Adam Thirlwell, 'On Muriel Spark', *Areté* 14 (2004), http://www.aretemagazine.co.uk/14-spring-summer-2004/on-muriel-spark/, accessed 14 November 2011.

57. Cited in Robert Hosmer, 'The Short Stories of Muriel Spark', in Alexander Malcolm and David Malcolm (eds.), *A Companion to the British and Irish Short Story* (Oxford: Wiley Blackwell, 2008), p. 457.

58. Spark, *All the Poems*, p. 59.

59. Martin McQuillan, '"The Same Informed Air": An Interview with Muriel Spark', in Martin McQuillan (ed.), *Theorising Muriel Spark: Gender, Race, Deconstruction* (Basingstoke: Palgrave, 2001), p. 215.

60. McQuillan, '"The Same Informed Air": An Interview with Muriel Spark', p. 213.

61. McQuillan, '"The Same Informed Air": An Interview with Muriel Spark', p. 216.

62. *The Complete Short Stories*, p. 184.

63. *The Complete Short Stories*, p. 379.

64. Muriel Spark, *Curriculum Vitae: A Volume of Autobiography* (London: Constable and Company Ltd, 1992; Harmondsworth: Penguin, 1993), p. 38.

65. Carl MacDougall (ed.), *The Devil and the Giro: Two Centuries of Scottish Stories* (Edinburgh: Canongate, 1991), p. 3.

66.   *Coriolanus* 5.3.34–7.

67.   Lodge, 'Marvels and Nasty Surprises'.

68.   Lodge, 'Marvels and Nasty Surprises'.

69.   Lodge, 'Marvels and Nasty Surprises'.

70.   Lodge, 'Marvels and Nasty Surprises'.

71.   Dean Flower, 'Looking Backward', *The Hudson Review* 51, 1 (1998), pp. 241-249.

72.   Stuart Kelly, 'Literary Exchanges: Scotland, Europe and World Literature', in Marc Lambert (ed.), *Discovering Scottish Literature: A Contemporary Overview* (Edinburgh: Published by the Scottish Book Trust on behalf of the Scottish Government, 2008), p. 34.

Fred D'Aguiar

Vulture Prayer Before Feast

Let us pray. Gods of takeout with bullet, rubber and steel, we give thanks to you for driving your wheels over this fur, flesh, blood and bone. Thank you for ironing flat so many small and sometimes not so small expressions of life. We praise your roads, our stomping grounds, our overladen tables at year-round banquets. Your modes of sport and transport convert living things for us to seek, find and devour. We promise to keep feeding as long as you keep supplying. If ever we do anything to offend you and make you stop your hunts and speeding give us due warning so that we may cease our transgressions into your fields of wheat and poppy, for we do not wish you to halt your bloody ways. We fly for miles chasing your fumes. May our feast never end. Amen.

Vulture Red Letter Day

Vulture days when she feels there's no wet·in the rain
When no two wingbeats sound alike

On such days she should just chill on a ledge and watch worlds fly by,
But no, she be vulture and she won't let nothing go nowhere,
Not without her say so.

In her mood she pushes from her perch into a breeze full of sweet things.

The moment she leaps she knows she made a big mistake
But one thing leads to another and other things take over

Before she knows it she's in the thick of a carcass set upon
By a crew drawn from miles around by a smell as rich as any seam,
Crack, crevice, fold, mold, groove.

She pins flesh with feet, lowers head, fails to hear the engine approach.

Vulture's Theory of Perpetual Return

I fly up and float on one wingbeat for as long as I can make circles
in the circling winds, I see the same things all the time and all that time
I see those same things differently.

The maze in the trees keeps me counting the trees in the maze.
Something in my gut tells me I am not what I eat, but what
I eat tells me not to believe everything my stomach tells me.

The meat I ingest, in all seriousness, is the meat I regurgitate.
The call I launch into the wind is a boomerang.
My shadow rides the plains below and thinks its shadow rides the winds.

My feather loosens like a human tooth in a human dead head.
I must be human too, destined for a hole in the ground if lucky,
luckier still, to grace a table for vultures known as the most enthusiastic of
eaters.

The lamplighter who lights all the lamps above
lights the lamps of my eyes and how that lamplighter douses
those cold flames so too my eyes turn dark.

I belong to no one and no one wants me when I am gone
to where I do not know, except for the sound just before
silence and the silence just after sound.

Vulture vs. Double Ugly

Double Ugly's single ear rocks hard
Against any advice from Vulture.

Double Ugly slurps his tea and lifts
His cup without holding out his pinky.

Double Ugly with two orange plaits down
His face, plaits more matted dreads.

Vulture averts her eyes when Double Ugly
Crosses her path and Vulture thinks

Ten times more than she says
For all her complaints come out plain.

She wants Double Ugly to improve
Little by little, not feel swamped.

But even those small amounts
Seem too much for Double Ugly

Who feeds one plait into his mouth
And nibbles while the other plait dips

Into his cup and appears to slurp
Along with Double Ugly's skinned lips.

Vulture keeps her cool as she basks
In her second place status on the plinth

Of ugliness in a world ruled by beauty
Seen by a beholder whose eyes are crossed.

Vulture Calypso

Vulture meet this poet with a capital P
Writing big-time poems seen on HD TV,
Poems with suffering as their main clause,
Poems so right-on his name's their cause.
He calls me (behind my back) a perve,
In reaction to V's LGBT and Q nerve.
P says poetry's a mask all poets must don,
But his entire face looks covered by a condom.
Vulture decide if that man's the last body
On earth, I go turn vegetarian or go hungry;
Though I got a stomach of acid and steel,
Me can't keep down a fat cat in newsreel.
I tired of his type of chat full of bluster
That can't measure up to what poetry muster.
The man busy so till being political,
His verse sound like an instruction manual.
He try so hard to kowtow to diversity,
He sound like a white paper in a university.
I wish I could tell him Vulture got a nose
For all good poems written in deep repose;
That Vulture knows a good smell from a bad one,
And that man's poems stream from his rectum.
Everything he write, banner must publish,
Including street corner stuff we labrish
That not worth the lick an' spit that make it
Since just beer, weed and rum proof it.
Who got courage to tell the poser the truth,
That a world without his posems still got Roots?

That we don't need another pontificating Bard:
Poetry got nuff fowl cock scratching backyard;
That the world got too much poems already;
That our art's diluted by his mock rock-steady.
He self-publish book and DVD each year,
A poetry Walla whose CV shows a career.
He must print everything that come to mind,
But most toilet paper can't stand the test of grime.
I write this because he behave like a high priest,
Presiding over a mediocre word feast,
Talking out both corners of his mouth,
Looking North but running poor poetry South.
If something fake somebody must say so,
That's why Vulture compose this calypso.
Don't mind my mix of satire and parody,
Not one drop of blood spilled from anybody.

Li San Xing

Kokerboom

'See this road?' Tobias asks, nodding at the trucks and petrol pumps blocking the view of the N1 through the window. 'It runs from Cape Town all the way to Cairo, man. All the way.'

Ben exhales through his teeth as Tobias rummages in his prehistoric beard, watching the coffee machine behind the counter gurgle and struggle with its latest assignment. 'You have to concentrate on that road, hey? Really concentrate. People think it's easy, one big road. Then just as they're thinking it, they fall asleep at the bladdy wheel.'

'They need someone to keep them awake,' Ben says.

'Yah, no kidding,' Tobias says. 'So the driver is kept awake trying to decide which is making him fall asleep more, the road or his daughter rabbiting on.'

Kay returns from the bathroom and they head for the racks of chocolate bars with names like 'TV Bar', throwbacks to an America of the '80s or '90s which even then would have been throwbacks to a crew-cut '50s.

'Have you ever known anyone who's fallen asleep on the way to this place?' Ben asks Tobias, trying not to notice the faintly erotic Os Kay is working her mouth into as she scans confectionery.

'Yah, man. Or worse, hit a buck. There's a whole shitload of massive great buck prowling around like idiots up there in the Karoo. Complete brainless idiots. Just last month a woman hit one, it went straight through the windshield.' He smacks his left palm with the back of his right hand. 'Like that. Finished. Both of them.'

'I'm good,' Ben says, palming away a Tempo bar from Kay.

'Take it,' she says. 'We might not be stopping for a while.'

Feeling something on his neck, Tobias turns to see two giggling black girls theatrically holding both glass doors open for their unimpressed young mother. 'What they should do,' he says, pulling up the collar of his fleece and turning back, 'is someone should just sit all those buck down and explain to them to stay off the fucking road. Really drill it into them. Stay off the fucking road, man. It's the only way.'

Outside, Tobias yanks open the back door of the pickup, propping it open with one arm so Ben can clamber in. He squints at his cargo, something occurring to him.

'Have you even seen photos of the place we're going, man?'

Ben shakes his head. Tobias reconfigures his green camouflage cap and grins, looking every bit the freshly defrosted caveman they are busy smuggling into modern society.

'Imagine the middle of fucking nowhere,' he says.

'OK.'

'Now imagine the place people who live in the middle of fucking nowhere go for some quiet time. That's where you're going.'

Tobias rarely mentioned him, this artist brother who lived out in the semi-desert. But for someone he supposedly wasn't speaking to, he called the workshop surprisingly often, Tobias abandoning whatever table, chest or cabinet they were making to go and sit on a toolbox with the receiver pressed to his ear, kneading his forehead and repeating the words I know. No, I know, David –

'Still keeping his phonebook in the fridge under the beers,' he'd joke after hanging up. And for the rest of the day Ben would notice excessive force in his master's hammering and sawing, an uncharacteristic impatience with stubborn timber.

The last time his brother called, Tobias was out and Ben answered.

'Tell Toby I'm sober,' said a slurred, metallic voice.

'OK, sure.'

'Tell him – why the hell are you speaking like that, man?'

'I'm Scottish, this is how we speak.'

A volley of laughter. 'Alright Billy Connolly, just – tell that to my brother, OK? Tell him I'm sober and I can finally leave town. Have you got that? William fucking – Wallace?'

'I got it.'

'Don't miss out a single word. His brother can finally leave town. And what does he think of that.'

About a week later Tobias answered the phone and sat on the toolbox kneading his forehead but hardly saying anything.

'Well,' he sighed after hanging up, 'my brother's dead. Pass me that panel saw, will you?'

At some point Ben wakes to find the undulating greenery of the Western Cape has been supplanted by a flat mass of brown scrubland. Assuming he has slept through hours of gradating landscape, he checks his watch and is amazed to find only an hour and a half have passed.

They pass through blink-and-you'll-miss-them towns, inexhaustible miles of nothing, muscles of mountain flexed and waiting in the distance but never reached. At one point the window behind his head rattles with Tobias' fist and he looks up from his book just in time to see a mob of baboons skulking along the roadside.

Eventually a sand-coloured municipality scatters itself unceremoniously around the pickup – not so much a town as a collection of streets the town planners seemingly lost interest in or died of boredom halfway through constructing. If it wasn't for the dragons, Ben would still hold out some hope that this isn't the place. But there they are, just as Kay described them, baring their metal teeth from the various shop fronts and cafés.

Tobias' brother moved out here when their mother was sick, and when she died he remained in her house, slowly pawning her belongings and adjusting his alcoholism to its new mountainous surroundings. They called the town 'sleepy' but he knew even the most dangerous creature had to sleep at some point. He resented the place from the start, even when it seemed intent on pleasing him by gathering enough ageing gay men, artists and new-age types into its fold for his amusement, every facet of his personality made flesh. 'It was like leaving a piece of food in a Petri dish,' Tobias said, 'and coming back to find a cushion of mould had grown around it.'

The days he wasn't working he spent wandering the sun-baked streets in his bare feet, boozing at the cafés and bars until he was drunk enough to hold forth on how he'd had his fill of this place and was leaving it forever; some mornings actually waking to find himself draped over a half-packed suitcase that he was careful to omit from his late-night rants.

'Saddle up my horse!' he'd shout. 'I'm getting out of this one-horse town, I'm taking the only horse and getting the fuck out.'

But five years passed and every morning the horse remained where it was, and there was either work to be done or a cold beer waiting for him in about thirty refrigerators around town, each of these bottles preying on his mind like a series of meetings his secretary had booked too close together.

The woman at the first café has been expecting them and is ready with the key for the padlock. Hugging Kay and Tobias repeatedly, she assures them David's spirit is 'free now' though she refers to his earthly form as 'such a free spirit'. She is sad to see the sculpture go and stands stroking its head like a lost dog she has to return to its owners. It is the size of a Labrador and constructed entirely from rusted scrap metal salvaged by David out in the semi-desert – old cans, car parts, bike spokes and gardening tools impressively welded into the shape of a snarling dragon that looks like it might come alive if you touched it in the wrong place.

Tobias is reluctant to make enquiries about David's welder until he can be sure who his friends are, but the woman proves to be an eager snitch.

'You've heard this guy's going around claiming he's the brains behind these beauties, hey?'

'Yah, we heard,' says Tobias.

'But so now David's friend Johannes tells me this welder guy's now started making his own dragons, yah. He's actually been trying to hawk one of these things around town. But apparently it's kak, man, really fucking awful.'

She insists on showing them David's table. It is on the far left of the veranda and distinguished from the other chipped wooden tables by a framed photo of a silver-haired man with smiling eyes and a small vase of red carnations surrounded by seven tea-lights, one of which has blown out.

'This was where he'd sit nearly every morning,' the woman says, welling up as she sets the dissident candle to rights. 'He'd sit here with his dirty old feet and order his usual, an ice-cold Black Label. I tried to find the coaster he used on the day he had the heart attack but the dumpster was too full.'

'Christ,' says Tobias, 'it's just tragedy after tragedy, hey?'

Before they remove the dragon, the woman asks them to take a photo of her sitting astride it, arms and legs outstretched in such exhilaration that it's clear this isn't the first time she has struck this pose. As they carry the sculpture to the pickup, Kay leans in towards Ben's ear.

'I think my uncle slept with her once by mistake,' she whispers.

If David lived in Venice he'd have trawled the canals for materials, his friend Janey tells them, but he was stuck here so it had to be the desert. 'Anything metal, the sharper the better. If it wasn't rusted, it wasn't ready.'

He never planned the sculptures, she says, just walked around his yard in his shorts, beer in hand, and selected the pieces. Three beers in, the welding began. 'He always bragged he could easily do his own welding, he just didn't want to fuck up his manicure. So he found the guy with the worst-looking, grubbiest nails and got him to do it.'

She tells them the story of the opening night of his exhibition, when a wealthy farmer expressed an interest in one of the dragons made from rusted implements foraged from his own farm. It was on for 6,000 rand and he offered to come and pay the following day but before he did, the gallery owner added an extra zero to the prize tag without David's consent. The farmer laughed in David's face, drove off in his jeep and David never spoke to the gallery owner again. 'He didn't even use the same colour pen.'

Being a big fish in small pond could be fun sometimes, but it didn't pay. One day, Janey says, David received a call from the district municipality who were interested in buying one of his larger pieces to install by the roadside outside Laingsburg. They agreed on 10,000 rand and sent him a contract in the post, but just as he was about to sign, he received another call. The municipality's lawyers were concerned that the sharp edges of the dragon might be a danger to the public – could he do anything to make it safer?

'So David suggests they place the sculpture somewhere higher. Perhaps up their lawyer's arse.'

The story goes that he disconnected his phone, ignored any letters with the municipality's postmark and a week later his friend Johannes went round to find him blind drunk in his backyard, spearing wine corks on the sharp points of one of the dragons, cracking open a fresh bottle whenever he ran out.

Their first sign of the welder: a loose chain coiled around a post outside a restaurant.

'When?' asks Tobias.

'Early this morning,' the man says. 'He was heading out of town – he came by, you know.'

'Why the hell did you give it to him, man?'

The restaurant owner shrugs, smirks, rubs his eye. 'He said it was his, he made it. I didn't know what to say.'

'You say no, man. David made this sculpture, you just did the fucking donkey work. Drive away.'

'Well, that's – '

'That's what you fucking say.'

'That's debatable, man, that's debatable.'

Ben's heart is pounding. 'My uncle paid for a service,' Kay says. 'The only thing this guy actually owns is the right to say he performed that service.'

'Yah.' The owner of the restaurant glances at Kay sleepily. 'But Monty was the one who actually sat down and made the things, you know? Your uncle mostly sat there watching with a six-pack. I mean if he wasn't already passed out.'

Tobias is chewing his bottom lip, hands frozen on his hips in perfect imitation of the restaurant owner. He looks over at the post with the offending chain, assuming the air of either a harmless bearded man admiring a prime length of chain or a dangerous bearded man seriously considering putting that chain to use. From the look on Kay's and the restaurant owner's faces, it is clear that nobody knows which of these men Tobias is.

They walk back to the pickup, their hands red but only with rust. There are bars on the windows here but no eight-foot gates or alarm systems like Ben is used to back in Cape Town. Crime here is low, Tobias tells him, because there's nowhere to hide. Run out into the semi-desert, they'll find you eventually. Every half hour or so a police car ghosts down the street, occasionally stops outside a shop. A policeman swaggers in, emerges with a brown bag of groceries, drives off.

The general consensus around town is that the coordinators of the artist-in-residency programme didn't know what they were asking when they offered to sponsor David on the condition that he quit drinking. Until then the only people who had ever wielded the Stop Drinking ultimatum were lovers he never cared enough about to try to hang onto. There was always some other pretty-boy willing to take his shit, but the chance to leave town forever, an all-expenses-paid apartment in Cape Town – that only came along once in a lifetime.

Everyone in town tells a different version of his attempts to sober up. Some have him reducing his alcohol consumption with surprising ease, whittling it down to one or two 'controlled' drinks every few nights. Others tell of a visible struggle, hard-won stretches of sobriety that collapsed into spectacular benders after only a few days. Many of the townspeople claim he turned on them in his final weeks, accusing them of deliberately keeping him drunk so he'd never leave. Some wonder if these quarrels were his lethargic attempt to leave the town piecemeal, fall out with the place person by person until there was no one left to sponge drinks off.

By the time they reach the bar for a late lunch, the stories have become downright implausible. One barfly in a Panama hat and swathes of beads tells them of the time David decided to 'do a Jesus', walk out into the semi-desert without so much as a sip of water in the hope of 'fasting out' his alcoholism.

'He was out there for about two hours before he stopped at the foot of a hill to rest on this rock, take a seat. So he looks down and he notices something shining, something shiny behind this rock. And he reaches down and – he can't fucking believe it, man – it's a six-pack of beer. Cooling in the shade of the bladdy rock, in the middle of the semi-desert. And not just any old beer: Black Label, man, his favourite fucking brand. So he sits there and polishes off every one of that six-pack and staggers back to town telling everyone he's met the devil and drunk him dry.'

Laughter. 'Yah,' says Tobias, 'I'll bet he accused you of leaving the beers out there for him to find, hey?'

'Ah, David knew he was never going to leave here. He knew,' says a large Afrikaans farmer sitting nearby. 'He was like a tent pin or something – if he left, the whole fucking town would collapse.'

'Yah,' says the man's girlfriend, 'or he would collapse.'

The man in the Panama hat stands and announces that everyone must drink a Black Label in honour of David. Tobias insists on paying for the round, and Ben knows this is as much of a tribute as Tobias is willing to pay his brother. There will be no sombre or heartfelt toast, no childhood story offering the locals a side of David they never knew; no staring off at the horizon or choking back tears at some long-forgotten photograph. If he regrets never burying the hatchet with his brother, Tobias will not show it. He is the first to finish his Black Label and immediately heads to the bar for the brand he was drinking before.

'I always think there's no worse place to stop drinking than a town in the middle of the desert,' the woman says. 'The desert, I mean – '

'Here, here.'

' – the desert itself is a great thirst that can never be quenched.'

'Shit, yah,' says the man in the Panama hat. 'I'll drink to that.'

Ben makes his way through the dusty lot to where the pickup is parked, unlocks the back door and twists it open. He has seen the other pickup lurking along the road, knows the man leaning out the driver's window is watching him. Shuffling inside, he finds the sackcloth bag of photos Tobias asked him to fetch and begins rooting needlessly through the pockets of his own backpack, stalling for as long as he can.

His hopes that the man will drive away are dashed by the suction-sounds of a car door opening and closing, the slow, uneven footsteps crunching towards him. From the corner of his eye he can make out a red checked shirt, arms knotted with tattoos.

The man is peering inside with bloodshot eyes, gesturing for him to open the sliding window. By the time Ben has fumbled with the latch and jerked it open, the man has forgotten what he wanted to say, is too preoccupied with the rusted dragons secured with rope inside the pickup.

'Howzit,' he says, breath rotten with alcohol.

'Hi.'

Steadying himself with a hand on the roof, he leans in for a better look at the sculptures, the little bed they have improvised for Ben out of rugs, duvets and pillow. He squints his eyes.

'Do you sleep in here, man?'

'Not really,' says Ben. 'There's no room for me in front.'

'But you're in here when the engine's on?'

Ben nods, tries to slow his breathing to a manlier pace. The man frowns, wiping his mouth with his hand and considers each dragon in turn, then Ben, like some discriminatory police lineup. He keeps his gaze fixed on Ben, a car shuddering along the gravel road behind him, wheels sneezing up dust.

Finally, he taps a finger on the pickup window.

'You shouldn't sleep in the back of these things, man. It's dangerous.'

'Dangerous?'

'The fumes – from the back, you know? They come up through the gaps and fill the whole inside, what's it – carbon – ?'

'Carbon monoxide?'

'Yah. It's dangerous, man, people die like this all the time.'

Ben clears his throat, nods at the window. 'I keep this open.'

'Well, yah,' the man snorts, mouth curled into a smile. 'People think that helps but all it does is create a kind of – a vacuum, you know?' He pushes his fist to his mouth to swallow a burp. 'I'm just saying, man.'

He glances behind him, swallows another burp.

'It's amazing,' Ben says, nodding at the scenery. 'Out here.'

'Yah.' The man nods, unconvinced, looking off at a path studded with fence posts, a quiver tree growing at a slope, thick white branches bunched upwards into pineapple rosettes. Then nothing but acres of scrubland, darkening sky and the mountains in between.

'Yah,' he repeats with a sigh, turning back. 'Anyway, man, I'm just saying – you should be careful.'

Ben nods. The man raises his eyebrows, tapping the window again to emphasise his point.

'OK, man,' Ben says, gives him the thumbs-up. 'I'll take care.'

The man returns the thumbs-up. 'Alright, man. Me too.'

He turns and lurches back to his vehicle. Ben watches him yank open his door, fumble with his keys and start the engine. Though the welder is showing every sign of leaving, Ben remains kneeling there until the pickup has rumbled around the corner and out of sight. It is a while before he can move his legs, wriggling out with the photos of their cabinetwork to show the barflies. They were only expressing polite interest, he thinks, as he lowers the pickup door. But until Tobias has peddled at least a chair or two, nobody is going anywhere.

The Parnok Poems

Marina Tsvetaeva (1892–1941)
translated from the Russian by
Christopher Whyte

The 22-year-old Marina Tsvetaeva already had a husband and a two-year-old daughter when in October 1914 her path crossed that of Sofia Parnok. Seven years her elder, also a poet, of Jewish origins, Parnok made no secret of her lesbian preferences. The two women embarked on a tempestuous relationship which lasted until February 1916. It was Parnok, suffering from a migraine, that Tsvetaeva reluctantly left behind, to go and read at a gathering of St Petersburg poets in December 1915, from which only Anna Akhmatova was absent. Unmentionable during the Soviet period, the relationship still causes embarrassment to some Russian scholars. Western readers will be struck by Tsvetaeva's utterly frank treatment of an experience which was fundamental for her, not merely in erotic terms. The wounds left behind resonate in an essay on lesbian love from the early 1930s, addressed to Natalie Clifford Barney, written in French in Paris, where Tsvetaeva had emigrated. For a while entitled 'A Mistake', 'With a Woman' (literally 'The Girlfriend') remained unpublished during the poet's lifetime. The cycle is here translated in full from the seven-volume edition of her complete works, along with four other relevant poems, the last of them addressed to Tsvetaeva's husband.

With a Woman

1

Are you happy? No need for an answer. You can't be.
Look, I never asked.
Lips in such numbers have pressed against yours
it's no wonder you're sad.

In you I find each tragic heroine from Shakespeare,
combined into one.
Young in years you may be, but your destiny's tragic –
with no saviour in sight!

Now you know it by heart, you've grown tired of repeating
love's recitative.
The ring of cast iron on your bloodless finger
says all that it takes.

Like a cloud filled with thunder, sin hovers above you.
I'm falling in love
with you. Why? For your burning sarcasm, because
you stand out from the rest.

The lives that we lead, and we two, are so different.
All paths lead through darkness.
You're a temptress of genius, yet not the less helpless
when struggling with fate.

I love you because I must bid you farewell,
demon with the steep brows,
because, as you rush to your grave, there's no hope
that you'll ever be saved.

Because of this trembling I can't put a stop to –
it must be a dream –
because, with a rapture I can't quite believe in,
you aren't a he!

October 16th 1914

2

Huddled beneath the woollen plaid
I relive dreams of yesterday.
What happened? Who came out on top?
Who was the loser?

I think it all over again,
the same torment returns.
In something I can't find the words
for, did love play a part?

Who was the hunter? Who the prey?
It's devilishly back to front!
How much did the Siberian cat,
that kept on purring, understand?

During that self-willed hand to hand
which of us kept within the rules?
Whose was the heart – yours, was it mine –
that soared into the sky?

Again the question – What was that?
Desire fulfilled? Pretext for pain?
I still can't work it out. Was I
the winner, or the loser?

October 23rd 1914

3

The thaw began today, I spent
a long time at the window.
My eyes weren't swimming, I could breathe
more freely, peace returned.

Who's to say why? I had grown tired,
perhaps, of turbulence
and felt no need to reach a hand
for that rebellious pencil.

I spent a while, equally far
from good and ill, in darkness,
drumming my fingers on a pane
that gave the faintest tinkle.

Nothing mattered much to me
or to the passers-by,
to puddles of mother of pearl
the skyline spilled into,

or to the songbird flying past,
the dog running intent.
Even the beggar woman's song
brought no tears to my eyes.

I'm mistress now in the sweet art
of learning to forget.
Some great feeling I cannot name
thawed inside me today.

October 23rd 1914

4

You couldn't bother getting dressed
or up out of your armchair.
Yet every day you had ahead
my zest would have made zestful.

You really drew the line at going
out so late into the cold.
Yet every hour you had ahead
my youth would have made youthful.

You did that all innocently,
what cannot be put right,
not realising I was your youth,
proceeding on its way.

October 24th 1914

5

Today, at eight o'clock, headlong
down the Main Lubyanka, like
a bullet or a lump of snow,
a sleigh shot past, going who knows where.

Laughter lingered in the air …
I couldn't take my eyes off you:
a shock of chestnut hair like fur,
someone tall sat at your side!

I'd already been replaced!
The sleigh ploughed onwards, carrying
the woman you love and desire –
one who's more desired than me!

'*Oh, je n'en puis plus, j'étouffe!*'
you cried in ringing tones, and tucked
her up in the fur travelling rug
with an energetic movement.

A joyous world, a gallant night,
presents toppling from your muffs …
Through the blizzard you two sped on,
your gazes meeting, and your furs.

A savage uprising occurred,
the falling snow piled white in drifts.
My eyes followed you for about
two seconds – definitely no more.

Without a trace of anger, I
smoothed the long fur on my coat.
Oh Snow Queen out of Andersen,
your little Kay had turned to ice!

October 26th 1914

6

She cries over the coffee grounds
all night, and gazes towards the East.
Loose and innocent, her lips
resemble some peculiar flower.

Soon crimson twilight will yield
its place to a young, slender moon.
You cannot guess how many combs
and rings you're going to get from me!

No one thinks about the young
moon among the branches there.
I'll give you such a lot of bracelets,
thongs, ear-rings on top of that!

From beneath its heavy mane
your horse's pupils sparkle brightly!
Your jealous fellow-travellers?
Swift-footed and pure-blooded steeds!

December 6th 1914

7

The snowflakes shone so merrily
on my sable, on your grey fur
as we looked for the gaudiest
ribbons in the Christmas market.

I gobbled no fewer than six
rose-coloured waffles – sugarless!
And petted every chestnut horse
to show how much I adored you.

Stallholders in billowing jackets,
red-haired, swearing, sold us trinkets,
stupid women wondered at
the fine, strange ladies down from Moscow.

When people started going home,
reluctantly we went into
the church. You couldn't take your eyes
off an icon of God's mother.

That frowning face was well-disposed
and haggard, set inside a frame
of podgy cherubs from the days
of the Empress Elizabeth.

Letting my hand slip out of yours,
you gasped 'I want her!' Then you placed
a yellow candle, with the utmost
care, inside its candle-holder …

Unpriestlike, with an opal ring,
hand of my whole catastrophe!
I gave you my word I'd come back
to rob the icon that same night.

Into the convent's guest quarters –
nightfall, din of pealing bells –
blissful as on our name-days
we clattered, like a troop of soldiers.

I swore to grow more beautiful
as I got older, spilled the salt,
while you were furious that the King
of Hearts should come three times for me.

Clasping my head in both your hands,
you gave each curl its own caress
then, with the little flower on your
enamel brooch, you chilled my lips.

I led your fingertips along
the contours of my sleepy face;
you teased me I was like a boy,
told me you loved me that way …

December 1914

8

Like a recent shoot, the neck
lifts without restraint.
Who can say her name, how old
she is, her land, epoch?

The sombre lips assume a curve
capricious and weak-willed
and yet the brow, like Beethoven's,
soars blindingly bright.

Her face's melting oval is
so pure it moves to tears,
her hand looks fit to grasp a whip,
its opal silver-framed.

That hand which ought to tense a bow
vanishes into silks,
a hand that is beyond compare,
peerlessly beautiful.

January 10th 1915

9

You go down your appointed path –
I won't attempt to touch your hand,
but my pain is too infinite
for me to treat you like a stranger.

My heart leapt towards you at once,
without even knowing your name,
I guessed it all, forgave it all –
Love me, I beg you, just love me!

Your pursed lips and your arrogance
pushed to the limits, make it clear,
the ponderous outline of your brow –
your heart's bent on taking by storm!

Your dress of silk, a black cuirass,
the gypsy hoarseness in your voice –
I love it all so much it hurts –
even that you're not beautiful!

No winter comes for looks like yours!
No blossom, you're a stalk of steel.
Knife-sharp ill-will personified,
what island were you kidnapped from?

Whether you use a fan or cane
to cast your spells, each vein, each bone,
each finger's grim outline exudes
feminine grace, a boy's defiance!

Parrying laughter with a verse
I proclaim to the world and you,
stranger with Beethoven's brow,
all that you hold in store for me!

January 14th 1915

10

How could I forget the scent
of 'White Rose' mingling with tea,
the Sèvres porcelain figurines
perched above a blazing hearth … ?

I was in a party dress
of ribbed silk with a hint of gold
while your black jacket was embroidered,
its collar finished off with wings.

I recall how your face looked
when you came in, without make-up,
how you rose, biting your finger,
head ever so slightly bent.

Your brow was like a general's,
your red hair like a weighty helmet,
no woman, yet not quite a boy –
in either case, stronger than me!

Without a pretext I got up,
people were surrounding us.
Provocatively, someone said:
'You two ought to be introduced'.

Taking your time about it, you
placed your hand in mine, and for
a moment a sliver of ice
dallied, coquettish, on my palm.

Someone looked disapprovingly,
I felt a skirmish imminent
where I lay, half-slouched, in my chair,
twisting my ring round and around.

You produced a cigarette.
I struck a match, gave you a light,
not knowing quite how I'd react
were you to look me in the face.

I remember how our glasses
clinked over a pale blue vase:
'I beg you, please – be my Orestes!'
And I offered you a flower.

Summer lightning in grey eyes.
Not hurrying about it, you
extracted from your black suède bag
a handkerchief – and let it fall.

January 28th 1915

11

Beneath the sun all eyes breathe fire,
one day's not like another.
Remember my words, if I'm ever
unfaithful to you:

It makes no difference whose the lips
I kiss in love's hour are,
it makes no difference who I swear
grim oaths to at black midnight,

saying I'll blossom like a flower,
subservient to a mother's will,
not turn my eyes to right or left
to look at anyone.

See this cross of cypress wood?
Take that as your sign
it's all a dream – whistle beneath
my window without fail.

February 22nd 1915

12

Close to Moscow the hills are wreathed in blue,
dust and tar in the air, a touch of warmth.
All day I do nothing but sleep or laugh,
recovering from the illness that was winter.

I return home as quietly as I can –
who cares about the poems I've not written?
Rumbling wheels, the scent of roasted almonds
matter far more than any four-line verse.

My mind's so empty that I feel light-headed,
given my heart is exceedingly full!
My days are like wave after small wave passing
beneath a bridge I stand on and look down.

A certain person's gaze is far too tender
in the caressing, barely heated air …
I've just recovered from the winter, yet
the illness that is summer has begun.

March 13th 1915

13

I say it over, as I count
how many days since we broke up,
since love's departure: I treasured
those hands, those very eyes of yours

which darted glances here and there
towards whoever caught their fancy,
at the same time demanding I
render account for every glance,

all of you, down to your three times
accursèd jealousy, which made you
– God sees it all! – exact reprisals
for every casual sigh I gave.

It wearies me, but I will add
– you needn't hurry to read this! –
that what was natural to you
grated constantly on my nature.

There's one thing more I want to say
– I count the days, I have the right! –
these lips of mine, till they kissed yours,
could have been a virgin's lips.

Until our eyes met, mine were bright
and unrestrained. I could have been
a five-year-old. Happy all those
whose paths never encountered yours.

April 28th 1915

14

Names have a fragrance like flowers that make you dizzy,
glances exist that are like dancing flames …
Mouths have recesses which, if you explore them,
are dark and labyrinthine, damp, profound.

Women exist whose hair is like a helmet.
Their fragile fans dispense catastrophe.
They're thirty years of age. What was it got you
interested in this girl's Spartan soul?

Ascension Day 1915

15

I want to ask the mirror, filled
with sleep and blurred half-darkness,
where your journey leads you, where
you rest your head each night.

Into view comes a ship's mast,
you walking on the deck …
Mournful fields as evening falls,
you shrouded in train smoke.

Twilit fields as the dew falls,
ravens croaking overhead …
To the four compass points, I send
my blessing upon you!

May 3rd 1915

16

What caught your fancy in the first
was her uncontested beauty,
the glint of henna in her hair,
the mournful lure of a Jew's harp,
horseshoes striking sparks from flint,
how neatly she leapt from her horse
and, in her semi-precious stones,
the curving patterns you discerned.

In the second – a different one –
the delicate arch of her brow,
the patterned roses in the silken
Bukhara carpets she possessed,
the rings she wore on all her fingers,
that single birthmark on her cheek,
the tan white lace could not conceal
and midnight London streets.

There was something about the third
that turned you on as well, I'm sure …

Has anything of me survived
in your pilgrim's wandering heart?

July 14th 1915

17

Remember – one strand of my hair
meant more than any other head.
Now go in peace – you too, as well,
and you, and you … All of you, go.

Stop loving me, all of you, stop!
Don't bend above me as day dawns!
That way I can quietly go
outside and stand there in the wind.

May 6th 1915

The clock has finished chiming – I
don't know the time.
In their sockets your eyes are huge,
rivers criss-cross the atlas of
your dress. It's hard
to make you out.

Above the porch next door the light
has been turned off.
Places exist where loving knows
no end. The outline of your face
terrifies me.

Within the twilit room night's in-
divisible.
Transfixed by moonlight, the window's
hollowed-out cavity could be
a block of ice.

'So you give in?' I hear you say.
'I didn't fight.'
Your voice is frozen by the moon,
it could be reaching me across
one hundred miles!

Between us a beam lifts itself,
moves with the world.
Enraged, your hair takes on a glint
of copper, with a dark red tinge –
unbearable.

History's progress is forgotten
in the progress
of a moon the mirror shatters.
Far off a horses' hooves are heard,
a creaking cart.

On the pavement the lamp's gone out.
Progress cut short.
Soon a rooster will proclaim the
time has come for two young women
to separate.

November 1st 1914

The moon is full, we wear bear fur,
the little bells dance playfully …
Now is the heart's most carefree hour!
The hour when I dig deep.

Wind in our faces makes me wise,
snow makes my eyes more kindly.
Bright on its knoll, the monastery's
a sacrament of snow.

You, friend, kiss the flakes away
from the sable on my chest.
I gaze on the village, the field,
the circle of the moon.

Our heads don't come together where
the coachman's back is broad.
I start imagining God, while
you're lost in your own dreams.

November 27th 1915

You could have been my mother in those days.
Feverish, insomniac light, I could
call on you from nightfall until dawn,
you were the light of my eyes in those days.

Look back upon them, you so rich in gifts,
those days on which the sun would never set,
days on which we played mother and daughter,
days when no sunset came, no evening fell.

Goodbye! I haven't come to trouble you,
I only want to kiss your dress's hem,
I want my eyes to look straight into yours,
the ones I kissed so often on those nights.

Some day I'll die, and some day you will, too,
some day I'll understand, you'll do the same …
Those days are irretrievable, but when
forgiving's feasible, we'll get them back.

April 26th 1916

I came to you at dead of night
as my last hope of help,
a mendicant, her origins
unknown, a sinking ship.

There's interregnum in my fiefs,
monks hatch their plots, while dog-
keepers wield power, and anyone
can don the emperor's robes.

Who didn't fight over my lands
or get my guards drunk? Who
didn't boil up their slops at night,
set the skyline in flames?

Upstarts and rapacious dogs
robbed everything I had.
I stand outside your palace door
begging, true emperor!

April 27th 1916

Martin MacInnes

Ascension Island

Islands are dramatic, places of plenitude and desertion, whole worlds and prisons from the world. Transient, threatened by submersion, they evoke the enigma of arrival and the urgency of departure. They are at the beginning of our stories, being compressions, indicators of worlds, useful to the scientist and the storyteller in theorising and pattern-seeking. Islands appear in early forms of fiction, slipping into the role of analogue for the isolated or eccentric mind, adrift from mainland, while in our grander visions of evolution we picture the first amphibious creatures – shelled, crablike – emerging after two billion years of marine transformation, scuttling onto beach, and it's like birth.

Ascension is 34 square miles of volcanic rock 700 miles NW of St Helena in the South Atlantic. It is the tip of a volcanic edifice built on the 6-million-year-old oceanic crust of the South American plate 2.2 miles below the waterline. Ascension is a British dependency, like the Falklands 3,800 miles SE, but unlike the Falklands Ascension is not physically located in a continent. Roughly equidistant to the west and east respectively are the coasts of Brazil and Liberia, and to the far north are the Cape Verde archipelago and the Azores.

The spinal mid-Atlantic ridge which extends from Greenland to Bouvet Island near Antarctica is the longest mountain range in the world. Peaks occasionally rise above the water as islands. It is a tectonically unstable region. Magma is constantly produced along the vents of the sea floor; the islands of the ridge are products of powerful volcanic bursts. Such uprisings are believed to have been instrumental in the production of the first cellular structures, and it is around such ridge sites still, several miles beneath the water surface, that approximations of this rudimentary life persist.

Ascension was 'discovered' twice, in 1501 by the Spanish explorer João da Nova Castella en route to India, and in 1503 by the Portuguese admiral Alfonso d'Alberquerque. Castella named it 'Conception' but it's d'Alberquerque's naming – he landed on Ascension day – that stuck. For the most part Ascension receives very little rainfall; it appears one of the most barren places on the earth. The lack of vegetation exposes the carved movements of eruptions and lava flow. The atmospheric conditions hold Ascension in a fossilised moment of trauma, as if the island has been suspended in an immediate post-eruption state. Perhaps encouraged in some oblique way by the metaphorical bombast of its name Ascension has a peculiar history of flight, or attempts at flight, from its harbouring of seabirds, the dramatic stories of its castaways and prisoners, to the launch preparations of NASA and the establishing of GPS.

Charles Darwin visited Ascension in 1836 aboard HMS *Beagle* as part of the survey of the world during which he gathered data towards the development of the theory of evolution by natural selection. He wrote about the island in his diaries and in *Geological Observations on the Volcanic Islands*. At Darwin's prompting the botanist J.D. Hooker, whose father was director of Kew Gardens, visited Ascension in 1847 and proposed to the Admiralty a method of artificially stimulating rainfall and thus carving the island into something more congenial to life.

Over a period of decades the Royal Navy brought ship after ship of trees from five continents and planted them on the slopes of the highest peak of Ascension. The trees would capture sea moisture and scarce rainwater carried in trade winds and in time add moisture and fertility to the ground.

The result: Green Mountain – Green Hill in Darwin's day – has been a success. It is the first example of terra-forming. Above the cinders, ash, and black-sand beaches at sea-level, the rising mountain gathers verdure. The southern and eastern slopes are covered by vast expanses of ginger and grasses, a distinct eco-system in total contrast to the surrounding land, an island itself within Ascension. The difference in the atmosphere and flora here and at sea-level cannot be overstated. Experiencing the discrepancy in a ten-minute car journey is distinctly unnerving, the nearest thing I can imagine to teleportation. Near constant SE trade winds lift the humid air up over the mountain where it cools and turns to fog and even rain.

Ascension owes much of its present form to the indirect influence of Napoleon Bonaparte, imprisoned in 1815 on St Helena. British fear of a rescue mission led to their occupying Ascension – the closest other land – and thus ruling it out as a base for any such escape. Later that century the island became a refuge for physically damaged soldiers. Garrison duties were assumed by the British Royal Navy. Ascension became an epidemic risk, with the threat of slaves and sailors spreading fever from the west African coast. On 'Comfortless Cove' cemeteries erected in the lava flow mark the deaths of scores of quarantined soldiers, shipwrecked on their patch of island. Ascension is still used as a setting for traumatised soldiers to convalesce.

Leendert Hasenbosch was born in the Hague most likely in the year 1695. Aged about eighteen, he joined the Dutch East India Company (or VOC, *Vereenigde Oost-Indische Compagnie*) as a solider stationed in Batavia (Jakarta). In the next several years Hasenbosch made two unusual financial decisions: in June 1718 he donated his entire outstanding salary to the building of a Lazarus house for lepers, and in August 1722 he again arranged for his outstanding salary to be donated, this time to a man in his home country named Jan Backner, of whom little is known.

The VOC records state that on 17 April 1725, midway through a voyage home, Hasenbosch was convicted of sodomy, and on 3 May was placed alone on the uninhabited island of Ascension. He was given a cask of an unspecified amount of water; onions, peas, chickpeas and rice; a tent, tarpaulin, bedding, clothes; a hatchet, two buckets, a tea kettle, a frying pan, a razor and a tinderbox. He set up his tent on the beach where he landed, today's 'Long Beach', then as now the primary nesting site for many hundreds of green sea turtles.

Hasenbosch's diary was found by the crews of the British ships the *Compton* and the *James and Mary* when they landed on the island on 19 January 1726 for repairs necessary to the *Compton*. The original diary is now lost, and what remains are at least partly fictionalised English editions. This is the long, full title of the 1728 edition, serving, as was contemporary style, as a synopsis:

An Authentick Relation of the many Hardships and Sufferings of a Dutch Sailor, Who was put on Shore on the uninhabited Isle of Ascension, by Order of the Commadore of a Squadron of Dutch Ships. – with – A Remarkable Account of his Converse with Apparitions and Evil Spirits, during his Residence on the Island. – and

– A particular Diary of his Transactions from the Fifth of May to the Fourteenth of October, on which Day he perished in a miserable Condition. – Taken from Original Journal found in his Tent by some Sailors, who landed from on Board the Compton, *Captain Morson Commander, in January 1726.*

So begins a riot of speculation and uncertainty. Daniel Defoe, who published *Robinson Crusoe* in 1719, was a Dutch speaker and is considered a possible translator of at least one of the English editions of Hasenbosch's diary. A transparently fictionalised edition was published in Dublin in 1730 – transparently, because it claims, among other details, that the original diary was found beside his skeleton; this is in direct contradiction to the reports given by Captains Mawson and Balchen of the *Compton* and the *James and Mary* respectively, as to their discovery of Leendert's possessions. It is the more sensationalised 1730 account that has regularly been cited, in modern times, as the 'authentic' diary. Another, even earlier edition has recently surfaced: *Sodomy Punish'd*, dated 1726, which contains further evidence of literary artifice, including direct allusions to the reader. It is as if modern literary theorists had contrived it: a performance of textual instability and factual uncertainty coinciding with the beginning of the English realist novel. Whatever doubt there is about the authenticity or validity of the existing editions of his writing, however, Hasenbosch is a historically recorded figure whose thirty years or so of life are touched upon several times by the records of the VOC. It is certain that he was alive, and it is certain that he was left on Ascension as punishment for sodomy.[1]

Reading the diary – the 1728 edition, which seems the least obviously adorned – is a peculiar experience. It is a guilty read: castaway literature is the laziest form of escapism. It is too big and broad a metaphor. And the diary is 'real' – Hasenbosch lived and suffered this, or at least an approximation of this. There is black humour in the limited, muted language he uses to record his thoughts on being stranded. This is the opening line of his first entry, dated Saturday 5 May 1725: 'By order of the Commadore and Captains of the Dutch Fleet, I was set on shore on the Island of Ascension, which gave me a great deal of Dissatisfaction ...' (Ritsema, p.51)

Historically, the defining characteristic of Ascension is its scarcity of water. This is also the main reason for its lack of history, its extending realm of pre-history, being one of the last places on earth to be settled. Hasenbosch found one small water deposit but was unable to track the larger source on what is now Green Mountain, a reserve that may have sustained him until sight of a passing ship. He expected to be saved, being told, possibly disingenuously by his Captain, that it was the season for South Atlantic passing trade and that therefore, it was implied, his punishment was not indefinite. This may have been one of the reasons Hasenbosch remained camped on the beach even after he had found a little water a distance away, and why he insisted on repeatedly wounding his feet by walking from that small water source to his camp across the sharp rocks in his shoes already ruined by the effort. It is a small island, but it took Hasenbosch sixty days to spot the goats, descendants of those left by sailors the previous century to add variety and year round availability of meat for passing ships. He might have spent more time following the goats in search of a greater water source. Instead, in his few and spare diary entires, he reports blankly of his trips across the rocks. (The briefness, and the subdued nature of the writing suggests the 1728 edition was not entirely fabricated.) He kills quantities of seabird and takes them with their eggs for food. By the end of August his water is exhausted, and he drinks from a mixture of urine, turtle-blood, and tea leaves. Later he folds his hands and digs inside a turtle searching for the bladder, which he bursts and drinks from. 'I am in a declining condition,' he writes. 'I am so much decayed, that I am a perfect skeleton, and can't write the Particulares, my Hand shakes so.' (Ritsema, p.105.) These are his three final diary entries: 7 October: 'My Wood's all gone, so that I am forced to eat raw Flesh and salted fowls. I can't live long, and I hope the Lord will have mercy on my soul.' 8 October: 'Drank my own Urine, and eat raw Flesh.' 9 October to 14 October: 'All as before.' (ibid.)

Apart from the cruelty, the first thing that strikes me about Hasenbosch's punishment, and other later punishments served by the VOC, is their theatre. We do not know who Hasenbosch's partner was and therefore we do not know how he was punished, but a common punishment for two men caught having sex at sea was to be tied – *back to back* – and thrown overboard. (It is possible, if his partner was a junior crew member, that Hasenbosch was made to watch him being thrown.)

This was not the only instance of castaway punishments for sodomy: two years after Hasenbosch was left on Ascension another VOC ship, the *Zeewyk*, exiled two boys (Ritsema, p.160). The sense of unreality evoked by this arbitrary punishment is notable in the language used in the transcript of the sentencing: 'we have resolved in council to place them apart from each other on the remotest islands,' (ibid. p.161). The idea of separating two boys finds an unbelievably hyperbolic expression in the placing of them each on an island remote from the other (tiny coral slates of mangrove, incidentally – lest we forget that people actually lived this theatre – only a metre above the waterline, absent of any food or fresh water), this giant physical gesture admitting a certain refusal to acknowledge internal lives. By placing them into a situation resembling myth or parable, these punishments dehumanise their subjects and degrade them into characters. These events occurred around the same time as the beginning of the novel in the English language; Defoe links them directly. Hasenbosch may have played a role in the popularising of prose fiction.

Of all the remote islands Ascension has the most particularly defined culture of the castaway. Through a series of coincidences, each, however, linked to the geological and meteorological conditions of the island, Ascension is connected to the beginning and development of the novel and to the theory of evolution by natural selection. Nobody has ever come from Ascension. It is always a destination, and always temporary. From the eighteenth century castaways and the ships that stopped to repair and gather food, to the British soldiers today who stop over briefly en route to the Falklands, Ascension has always been useful to people who are going elsewhere. Citizenship is impossible. Today the administration of the island turns over the transient population of service workers from St Helena ('the Saints'), British and American soldiers, research scientists (biologists and astronomers) and communication engineers every two years. The law has it that nobody can become familiar with Ascension. There is no retired population and few children. Leisure is not presumed, though there is a golf course ('the world's worst green') and a football pitch, and European businessmen occasionally base themselves there for game fishing. There is little in the way of medical facilities. Birth was late in coming here, and it has never been encouraged. It is assumed that people won't be born on the island and neither will they die there. There is no *human generation*. RMS *St Helena* and military aircraft artificially introduce people to the island, as the island's flora was artificially introduced and as the cats that have devastated the once abundant populations of seabird were artificially introduced.

In 1899 the company now known as Cable & Wireless Worldwide first used Ascension as a hub from which to spool out underwater cables linking continents. The island remains a nexus of communication equipment. One of five ground antennae used in the operation of the Global Positioning System (GPS) is based on Ascension. Contract workers man the massive satellites that relay the BBC World Service transmission to South America and Africa (as well, an Irish construction worker told me, as operating as a pair of ears for the secret service), and workers in bright orange boiler suits blast into the cinder-ground, planting further communication masts and towers. The majority of the island is strewn with elaborate meshes of pylons and aerials, sparse, unmanned metal frames that lean over plains of rubble and black rock. The population drifts at an ever-revolving 800. Today there are sheep – no goats – and a score of wheezing feral donkeys, indulged as an eccentricity (being useless since the introduction of cars) which appear from time to time in the main settlement of Georgetown, a collection of white pre-fab block buildings and a stone church by Long Beach, the same beach that Hasenbosch slept on for six months in 1725.

Ascension has a history with space, distance, silence. It is one of the most prestigious locations from which to watch beyond the earth. In 1877 astronomers on Ascension viewed the Opposition of Mars with heliometers, chronographs, chronometers and reflecting circles. The successful creation of Green Mountain has been noted as a possible example for colonising Mars. In 1966 NASA built an integrated Apollo and deep-space station on the island, looking up to extravagant and troubling flight paths. The particular site within the island was chosen for the cocoon of volcanic peaks which isolate the communication equipment from radar and radio-frequency interference. The station was abandoned in 1990; cabins and rock foundations remain, feathered by grass.

I visited Ascension in April 2007. The young soldiers dozed and read fantasy fiction on the seats and floor of Brize Norton airbase, Oxfordshire. The service crew on the plane was from Oklahoma, and I remember they spoke unclearly, their safety demonstration was a parody, they acted their roles slowly and with fatigue, and the plane was in a state of disrepair.

I was excited and unsettled about entering into a fiction. I thought

I would walk around the whole island. I badly burned my feet on the first day's walking. Blisters significantly increased the size of my feet and while it was painful to walk it was more painful still to stop and stand. I remember clearly watching the blood congeal in the fatty lumps on my feet the one time I was forced to stand still: taking a piss.

I tried, for years, to fictionalise Ascension, but I was unable to do it. The atmosphere of sterility and barrenness, the silence and peculiar architecture, the toy-town names of the island's features, all against an astonishing black cinder landscape orchestrated by hundreds of aerials, masts and satellites – all these monuments to communication – clearly set up the perfect zone in which to put a plot. Everything in the island is potentially significant, everything a symbol awaiting its referent. The pregnant green turtles emerge in rows at night out of the impossibly violent breakers on Long Beach, huge black lumps of coated flesh that take an age to find a distance safe from the reach of the water to dig holes and lay their eggs. There is no light on the beach and it is shocking to suddenly become aware of the presence of these shapes humbly spilling out of the black waves after a journey of months across the Atlantic to give birth, as if nostalgically, where they were born. And then they return, again in inexorable lines, into the violence of the water – it looks absolutely like suicide, these ungainly creatures pushing themselves into thrashing nets of dark – where they are transformed into elegant and extended sea creatures.

The problem, perhaps – for me, anyway – with Ascension as fiction is that it is too loaded with symbols and metaphors. It is overweight, already too fictional to be treated. Ascension has something of the child's imagination about it; a child's idea of an island, which routinely runs out of certain foods, whose features have such names as 'Donkey's Plain' and 'Comfortless Cove', which still generates a significant proportion of its income selling stamps, and whose law – ironically, given the biological significance of the area – frowns on the act of reproduction.

What is Ascension? This question is worth invoking in an attempt to explore the idea of beginnings. To attempt to regroup, restate: had the VOC been influenced by Defoe? *Robinson Crusoe* may have inspired the melodramatic imagination of the VOC – putting men alone on islands – while these real instances of castaways may have given the translator additional material with which to fictionalise. So: the original English novel is repeated on an island an account of which is translated/rewritten (perhaps) by the author of the original novel. Defoe's fiction anticipates Hasenbosch's experience. Like Ascension, Crusoe's island features goats and several hundred turtles. Both protagonists shelter on a tent by the beach. Crusoe, however, unlike Hasenbosch, is saved. He finds fresh water and domesticates the island; much of the book is an unfurling of agriculture over wilderness. Hasenbosch is unable to farm. Crusoe becomes lord of the island. Hasenbosch's story is flatter and darker and alone. He is undramatically trying and failing to provide for himself and stay alive.

The ruins of the NASA site, the barren basalt planes and networks of pylons and towers underscoring the vertical jungle of Green Mountain, the rumours of the multitudes of seabirds who had colonised the island in prehuman times and, most startlingly of all, a particular detail in Hasenbosch's castaway story, suggest that there is something yet in the contradictions and dislocations of Ascension worth pursuing.

Despite intensive searches by the crew of the *Compton* and the *James and Mary* on the island of Ascension in January of 1726, no trace of Leendert Hasenbosch's body was found.

Note

It is possible, though highly unlikely, that there was no 'original' diary – and that the crews of the *Compton* and the *James and Mary* having colluded to invent it for financial gain. Both ships' logs record the discovery of a diary among other possessions on the beach.

Sources and Further Reading

Darwin, Charles. *Geological Observations on the Volcanic Islands*. London: Smith, Elder and Co., 1844.

Ritsema, Alex. *A Dutch Castaway on Ascension Island in 1725*. All references are to the second edition published independently by Ritsema in 2010 via lulu.com. Ritsema's book – which includes the entire script of the 1726 and 1728 translations of Hasenbosch's diary – is itself an extended translation of an investigation by the Dutch historian Michiel Koolbergen into the identity of the 'Dutch castaway'.

Ciaran Berry

On the Jukebox of the Morning After
& the Night Before

(for C.G.)

Like the last of our moving statues stepping down
from her grotto somewhere just south of Kinvara
or Skibbereen, you were pure retro in your paisley shirt
and bell bottom jeans when you came to me
the morning after or the night before, a moon
of sweat waxing below your left oxter
as you pressed the distortion pedal to the floor
and set to working your black Stratocaster
on our last night at Kelly's of Portrush, where
the ravers, all whistles and day-glo gear,
were busy at forgetting on the dance floor
next door, and the just down from Larne
and Portadown bikers kept shouting out
for something by The Stones before Brian Jones
was found perfecting the dead man's float
in his own swimming pool. Where after a full set
and three encores, the paraplegic ex-drummer,
who'd spent the night hitting the high hat
and snare he'd conjured out of air, trundled
over to tell us we could make it somewhere
if you would only choose between singing
and playing, playing and singing, which, here,
might stand in, like a stand in bass player

or a group of backing singers, for the crooked line
between a body and a mind, the one demanding
the ambidextrous command of half a dozen
or a dozen strings, both necks mounted,
let's say, on the '63 Gibson where you'll learn
your way between the fury and the calm,
the sink or swim, of 'When the Levee Breaks'
and 'Stairway to Heaven'; the other a much
more elusive thing, the body asked to wrap itself
around what, given your taste for the vintage,
for the bygone, would always be the words
of a dead man or a dead woman locked
in the circumlocutions of melody, the strophe
of verse, the chorus's antistrophe. Singing
and playing, and your being caught between the two,
like the stubbed out cigarette of our misuse,
caught as we were on the far side of the border
in a seaside town at the dead end of winter,
across from the battened down funfair
and the boarded up arcades, between
a barbershop and a Chinese Takeaway, where
the carp would soon be floating on their sides.
Where, between our drummer's count outs
and count ins, we thought we spoke in tongues,
setting fire to ourselves and to our instruments
with whatever burned the belly or the lungs,
the bitterest of westerlies sweeping in under the door,
like the cold shoulder the locals were said to offer,
raising the carpet from the sitting room floor where
our mismatched tribe would gather and re-gather
with a carryout of apple schnapps and rotgut cider,

with twenty Silk Cut Purple and ten Carrolls Number 1,
to argue over what ought to be played or replayed
on the jukebox of the night before or the morning
after, the squeaky heads of the cassette player
circling towards the solo Hendrix plays holding his lips,
as if over a mouth organ, over a sheet of cellophane
stretched across a comb, to mimic traffic
moving in shifts and swathes cross-town;
the right arm of the record player cresting towards
the sound of feedback rattling the tympanum
in the wild man's wild live version of 'Wild Thing',
where, wearing a frilly orange shirt, a gold
earring, he pours a can of Three-in-One oil
over his guitar's flamed maple and sets it alight
as if to explain something about beauty, how
the young will always immolate themselves,
burning from the inside so that nothing can be done,
something kindling in us that will seek out
its flame. Like the tablature for a pentatonic scale
I could never learn, the first three songs on a mix
tape you made me once, or the drunk I awoke
to find one night standing at the end of my bed,
come in through a backdoor left unlatched
to ask after a ghost who'd once rented him a room,
it all comes back, it won't leave me alone –
the smashed glass and ashtrays of lost time,
of our best bare-arsed attempt at real living,
so wound up we were the nickel in the string
before it snaps mid-tune, bringing to an end,
instrument by instrument, microphone by microphone,
whatever is being played or being sung.

The Astor Cinema

The first time I saw the female form almost exposed
was from the front row of the Astor Cinema.
As the actress stepped out of her tent in *Spies Like Us*
to stretch, snowsuit unzipped down to her booted feet,
it was the sudden, laden hush of falling snow,
it was the moon aglow over three fields fresh from the plough.
What your mother can't see, your mother doesn't know,
my father's silence seemed to say as we drove home.
That for our best behaviour, he'd promised *Ghostbusters*
no longer seemed to matter. The ark was now ajar,
or at least the ark of the Playtex Cross Your Heart.
I could bear even the fetor from the men's room
as I peeked up from behind my Maltesers
and, puce-cheeked, stared through the male lead's binoculars.

At Ballyconneely

'On 2 August 1908 a mirage of a faraway city was seen at Ballyconneely, on the Connemara coast. It was described as a city of different-sized houses, in different styles of architecture, and was visible for over three hours' — *Foster's Irish Oddities*

Who knows, if you look long enough,
what might blossom up out of the spume?
Dead man's fingers, gutweed, Neptune's necklace,
plastic bottles from Vladivostok and Gdansk,

or an entire town, floodlit at midnight
and, it appeared, floating out there beyond
the range of cormorants, the black
and whiskered buoys that turned out to be seals,

while the whole village gathered at the pier,
puffing on clay pipes, consoling grandchildren,
until someone said it must be New York
and someone else Boston, from where

her stunned sister had just sent a letter home
folded three times over a lone dollar
and describing the taste of a Bartlett pear,
the man from Clare she'd met at a church dance.

The freckled Conroy twins stood holding hands
as if their drowned father's return
was imminent, as if his upturned currach
had just beached somewhere out there,

and not gone down broken among whale
graveyards, wrasse and mackerel shoals.
While the widow Lynch dropped to her knees,
fingered her beads, and swore the saviour

would walk soon again upon the water,
come ashore here to black tea, brown bread,
sean nós singers, to a landscape stone-
pocked and strange as the red face of Mars,

or the dirt floor of that half-made heaven
in Signorelli's painting where, legged
and armed again, naked and toned,
the dead welcome one another into an afterlife

that appears much the same as the before.
No one said mirage. No one said a reflection of the moon.
No one said Shangri La. No one said Xanadu.
That's not the sort of people that they were.

And because the gnarled, barnacled rocks lurk
just below that broken stretch of coast,
no one dared take a boat out there before dawn.
For the meantime, for their own separate reasons,

those Maddens, Mealys, Conroys, and McLanes
waited for something, not quite sure
whether they were waiting for the seraphim
to fill their dimpled cheeks and blow their horns,

the groan of thole pins and the splash of oars
that might welcome some hero out of folklore home,
or the propeller drone as a biplane bearing
Alcock & Brown came down out of cloud,

swooped shrike-like towards heather and gorse,
the whisky that kept them warm still wet
on their breaths, and on their tongues,
news of the new world, salt from Atlantic foam.

Alice Thompson

Burnt Island
An extract

Rose leapt up. 'I'm going for a swim.' And she disappeared behind the dunes.

Max waited for her to reappear but when she didn't, decided to explore the dunes. After ten minutes of walking he came upon a circle of five standing stones. One of the things he liked about ancient monuments was their imperfection but as he approached the circle, he saw the circle was so symmetrical it seemed abnormal. He remembered how difficult it had been to draw circles in school art lessons. How they had curved or turned into ovals or misshapen bumps. Only Giotto could draw a perfect circle. He went up close to the stones and saw ancient lettering on them but the script was indecipherable.

Max turned to look at the dark blue sea but when he swung round again one of the stones had moved out of the circle, to make a disjointed line. It must be the angle, he thought, he must have changed his position while looking at the sea, but whichever way he leant, the stone had visibly broken the circle. The circle had been perfect and now it was not, as the sea ebbed and flowed on the beach.

Max felt deeply disturbed because disbelief had become mixed with the evidence of his own eyes. A trauma of perception that seemed to tear at the shimmering membrane of his life through which reality was reassuringly obscured like shadows in a cave. But now the membrane had torn, reality was peeping through, bright and vivid and hard. That was the trouble with reality, he thought, it was just too real for him.

He tentatively went up to the shifting stone. It was entrenched in the grass and earth and sand, as the others were. But it was no longer part of the circle.

No soil had been disturbed, there were no lines in the grass, no wheels. Had he been mistaken? Had his perception of a perfect circle of standing stones been wrong. He walked back in the direction of the picnic site, took a deep breath and looked back at the stones. The stones stood like lonely sentinels in the distance. They were standing in a perfect circle.

He returned to their picnic site on the beach to find Rose standing there wearing a scarlet one-piece swimming costume. There were no details on her costume, no frills or metal hoops. She didn't need any adornment. She adorned herself. The surface of her was very smooth.

He remembered teaching Luke, as a toddler, to swim in the sea, remembered his son's unadulterated joy at being in the open water, his ecstasy at having having his father's complete attention for once. Max's sense of Luke's happiness was so acute it had turned his breath to glass.

Rose ran down into the sea and he watched her swim for a while. Her pale body bobbing up and down like a porpoise between the waves. She then waded out, dripping wet and walked up the beach as if enjoying every step her foot took in the hot sand, every caress of the cool breeze that wafted onto her skin, every sensuous drop of salt water falling from her limbs. She walked right up to where he was lying on the sand and stood above him, the expanse of her pale skin like a cloud, her costume like the blinding sun. Her body looked like it had been carved out of the situation – the ancient stones, the blue sky, and the distant roar of the Atlantic. She lay down beside him on her side, her body arched.

'I've come here to write,' Max found himself saying, plaintively.

'Of course you have,' she said. Just then they heard voices. Rose leapt up and quickly pulled her dress on over her head. A man was approaching them, his fair hair glinting in the sun. It was Ryan.

'I was looking for you, Rose, what are you doing here?' He took her hand abruptly.

He was staring at Max suspiciously.

'Just having a picnic.'

Ryan quickly flashed a smile and tugged at her gently to lead her away.

Max, clutching around in his head for some words to delay Rose going, said, 'Anytime you want me to take a look at your writing …'

'Oh, yeah. Thanks Max.'

She gave him an innocent smile.

Max watched as the two young lovers disappeared down in to the village. He felt, mingled with his sadness at Rose going, a fleeting fear. Fear for himself at what would happen if his new book was a failure. Could he keep his promise to himself that he would then give up writing altogether? Would he be able to ? Writing was his life blood, his life's work.

He walked back towards the house. He could hear the Atlantic beating on the shore. A blustery wind had started up. He looked down below and saw the small pier he had arrived at – Natalie could have left there by boat and no one would have seen her.

On returning to the huge living room he looked for any photographs of Natalie on the walls or cabinets. But there were just photos of James at triumphant moments of his life – graduating from Cambridge, winning the Pulitzer. He hadn't changed much – extremely handsome men or beautiful women weren't ravaged by age as much as normal people.

He wondered how Natalie had gone missing. Surely on an island it would be difficult to disappear without someone noticing? Surely someone must have seen something suspicious? It was also odd that there was no record of her anywhere in the house. Her absence was palpable. Why had James expunged her so thoroughly? Had James' grief been so overwhelming, he couldn't bear anything that reminded him of her?

***

Max thought he would sell his soul to the devil to write his new horror book, if only the devil existed, if only he could just bump into him and get him to make an offer. At dinner, waiting for James to come down, he wondered what the devil would look like. Plausible, without doubt plausible. He would, like an artist, have to convince you of his lies. He would have a sense of the absurd. Especially the absurdity of his own existence.

Why was he thinking these nonsensical thoughts, he wondered? He didn't believe in the devil. He hardly believed in evil – just the banality of man. But evil per se in the shape of an archetype … ? It was this island making him think these thoughts. That roaring of the sea was playing with his mind. It was like a hungry monster crying out for his soul and his sanity.

Ironically, the only time Max felt the devil's existence was when he was writing. Sometimes when working on a novel he felt like he was locked in battle with a dark force which was helping him cover the blank pages with the words of convoluted dreams. A kind of gibberish which he took down like dictation in his first draft and only after subsequent drafts could translate. But his new horror bestseller would have nothing to do with satanic creativity. It would be written by the rational god of market forces.

Max rubbed his eyes vigorously. When he lowered his hands, there was James sitting at the end of the table, smiling and avuncular.

'You know, Max, this is your chance to write the book you've always wanted to write on Burnt Island. Without compromise. Have you any idea how impressive you are? The way you keep writing the types of novel you do? Against all the odds? In spite of so little reward? What integrity that shows, what belief in your art?' Max hadn't told James about his secret plan to write a bestseller because he knew any respect James had for him would have evaporated like a snowflake on the back of his hand.

'You mean write a book like my other ones?'

You can go even further.'

'Make them even more unreadable?'

'Unreadable only to: the prejudiced. The lazy. The loveless.'

Max was moved – few people had shown such faith in him, certainly not his ex-wife, his ex-publisher, his agent. Only Luke had shown unswerving faith in him, had told him a number of times, 'Soon, Dad, you will make some money.'

'How do you know, Luke?'

'Because it's only fair. You work so hard. You work through the night.'

Max hadn't the heart to tell him fate was nothing to do with fairness, nothing to do with love. Of course as Dot and as publishers constantly whispered in his ear, 'No one is making you do this.' But they didn't understand. Of course someone was making him do this. He was making him do this.

Listening to James' encouragement, Max was even more confused about his plan to write a horror. Here was James, one of Britain's greatest contemporary writers, telling him to keep the faith. To do what he had always done, but more so. Max felt torn. He had been set on his path and now wondered whether it had been the right path. He rallied – he must remain focused. His bestseller must appeal to millions, be full of sex and terror and character development.

The two men tucked into his rhubarb crumble, deliciously sweet and tart at the same time.

'So do you have any ideas for your next book?' James was asking.

Max thought fast. 'I'm planning to use the symbolism of Burnt Island to explore our fear of mortality.'

James looked impressed and nodded.

'I love your use of symbolism,' James said.

'Readers don't.'

'Who cares about the readers? James Joyce said he wrote for only one reader. The ideal reader.'

It was all very well for James Fairfax to be saying this, thought Max, with his million bloody readers.

'The trouble with one ideal reader,' Max said, 'is it means only £9.99 for two years of work … There is something odd about this island though,' he added.

'Odd?' James looked surprised. 'In what way?'

'I don't know. Things don't seem quite right.'

'You mean in order.'

'Things seem slightly slanted to one side. A foot too much to the left.'

'And you want to straighten us up?'

'I'm hardly the person to do that.'

'You're off-centre.'

'Exactly.'

James laughed, the candlelight flickering between them. Max felt they were experiencing a strange correspondence of minds.

'It was odd. I was in the dunes the other day. Amongst the standing stones,' Max said.

James looked amused. 'Ah yes, the standing stones. Ancient pagan rites took place there many years ago, I believe.'

Max hesitated, wondering whether to say what had happened. Encouraged by James' expectant mood, he said, 'It was bizarre. Mad. I thought one of them moved.'

James looked at him, suddenly alert. Had Max stumbled on a supernatural event, or was James thinking he had gone mad?

James said quietly, 'Trick of the light, old boy, I'm sure.'

'No one's ever mentioned to you anything like that?'

'You mean a standing stone going for a walk? No I can't say they have. I think I've read somewhere it means someone has borne witness to a loved one in danger. But done nothing to help them. Instead they've walked away. Had you had one too many drinks perhaps?'

'Anyway, it's what I thought I saw.'

'That's what I like about you, Max – the way you think. You're an original. It's all your imagination, Max – best put it into one of your books.'

'Life is all built on illusion, isn't it? An illusion of our immortality. How can we go round every day knowing we're going to die? We're prey to illusion – it's essential to our wellbeing. We must of necessity have our illusions. We just all have various illusions to different degrees. As a writer you'll always suffer from a greater degree of illusion than most people.'

James the man of letters, looked at him his eyes twinkling in the candlelight. The white damask tablecloth only slightly stained pink where some drops of his red wine had fallen.

'I'm going to bed now,' James said. 'You're welcome to stay up for a while and muse.'

Max remained sitting at the table, listening to the sea crashing against the rocks, outside the luxurious glass box he was in. The good food in his stomach, the fire burning in the grate, his pleasant feeling of inebriation, contributed to a sense of contentment he had not felt in a long time. Just then there was a scream. Max was sure it came from somewhere in the house. It had been a piercing scream – hardly human. It must have been the cry of a fox. He began to feel uneasy. The room was exposed by the large glass windows overlooking the sea.

That night he had a dream a succubus came to him. She was voluptuous with dark hair and rode astride him violently until he came, panting and sweating. Her breasts were round and high like the distant moon shining through his window in the black sky. He woke drenched in perspiration, his and hers, heat pouring through every inch of his body as if his entire skin had been scalded in boiling water.

Charles Doersch

For Sean
Counter-Love

First light pearling down the face of Mt. Prow
now comes on openly for us
       swelling through the forest
the far side of this alder and cinquefoil meadow.

       Around us, lichened views,
grass-lashed wind, a cloud's avalanching fringes,
barks of the glacier scoring daily inches,
surf sounds of fir and spruce.

We're early for this earliest dance.
Each flower spark is waiting for the sign
       (cue the mosquito's whine),
when here through sere ungraspably clear distance

he comes. The sun, taking up his station,
       hot in the ways of grace,
dumps flagrantly on earth and space
quickening without calculation.

Right there a whole tree catches crosswise
in a blaze. Tree after tree, rootstock to head

— the shabby, the perfect, the dead —
go up alight before our eyes.

He dawns on us, as well. We burn,
wallflowers at someone else's ball no more,
so with kinnikinnick and the vetch we adore
   we take a light-heeled turn.

   What thanks we give
is peeling back petals, going at it, ovule,
root, fruit, and all, all grateful
in this oldest of Amens — to more than Live,

but Flourish and be fruitful, right,
   in whatever fashion
we have. And we have chartreuse-sequined aspen
clones who stipple us like trout in light.

Shivering against you this passed hour,
now that sunup's come and the day's hot on us,
for all our childless love has brought us,
   I bring you this, my flower.

Tony

(1997–2000)

Black firs and moon snow.
Puzzle chiaroscuro.
Fox tracks gone up hill.

Watching for him still.
Still dark clarity, and deep.
Still child, not asleep.

How Should We Pray?

Gospel of Thomas 6

Not that they take even the least
thought (how then action,
dear heart?) to each dissolution,
or to what degrees their endless
end products last.
How could they? Each cloud produces
of necessity, its lovelies
an unending stream of pointless
elaborate irreplaceables
the universe reduces.
That selfsame universe, just as we
speak now (there, out the window, see
across the hospital smokestacks?), looses
a milky mile-long slurry
of what, I think, are surely,
were purely
crystals.

Cloisters

Deep asters with enough black light
In what seem petals they ignite
Sending up flames no human sees
Smoking with bees

Diving face down in the tangled
Florets of the disks spangled
Hungrily with licks of swollen
Moments of pollen

In the close heat of the garden where
Two nuns bend their covered hair
Over dark bunches of fuming stars
Close mouths ajar.

Colin Graham

Portion

None of these things work now. These things that said of themselves, 'this is the future, here and now', none of them work anymore. When I first started travelling on this train, commuting once a week, I'd watch the pensioners, all on their free travel passes, nervous about the electronic buttons which OPEN | CLOSE | LOCK the toilet doors. They'd press the buttons, hard. Some would forget to LOCK and be caught, stooped over the bowl, as the double doors opened, wide enough for a wheelchair to get through. Now the LED sign indicating the next stop falters and flashes, gets stuck at … *CENTRAL* … The line of bulbs that is meant to light on the map to show where we are, between Belfast and Dublin, is dark. And so I don't trust the toilet doors any more than they once did. This electronic future, already worn out.

When I commuted for the first year it was all just right. The train was new and the journey was remaking me. Belfast for work, Dublin for weekends. I revisited the city of my childhood, just as it began to imagine itself finally grown up, while for love, and life, and holidays, I went to the city of my lover, and she having just returned there, from England. I wasn't quite sure exactly where I was living but everything was new and old at the same time, paralleled and connected by the journey. Then came the second year of being the urbane, detached commuter. I would be reading and reading, early morning and late evening, coming to know the pace of the journey, seeing the seaside towns between Dublin and Drogheda growing into each other. The sound of the track and the passing of the miles and the turning of the pages were all in time to the landscape's steady change.

After two years, the weariness set in. The fabric on the seats, once reassuringly business-like, took on the feel of sandpaper. The conversations around me sounded louder and increasingly pointless. The inanity of mobile phone chatter − 'I'm on the train', 'I'll meet you at the station', 'I'll be home at 9'. I began to fall asleep during the Friday evening journey back to Dublin, head against the cool glass. I would wake up, startled by my own jerking nod of half-sleep, staring into the darkening void, at dusk, near Newry, where the railway bridge, like in some thirties' train movie, stretches improbably over a gorse-strewn valley. Then the morning train became a time of dry-lipped slumber, interrupted only by the braking stops. Opening my eyes, with blurred vision, to see the station sign for PORTADOWN, herald of a vista of wire and soiled concrete, and on the drop-down table in front of me my mobile phone, networked-switched, proudly announcing itself, with no irony, as ORANGE-UK.

Today I'm travelling this track again, but in a leisurely way. A bit of work, 'research' as it's called, in Belfast, and then back to my now full-time home in Dublin. This train has always had a particular Friday-evening character. Groups of women, of various ages, dressed sparkingly, drinking gingerly, talking more loudly the further away from Belfast they move. Released from the drag of the everyday, they glide towards 'shows' in Dublin − musicals and boybands. On some weekends there are international rugby fans, sometimes international rugby players, surprisingly not in first class. And there are sporty boys with low-slung, ugly GAA bags, the shapes of boots and shin pads stretching the fabric.

Usually I go for the privacy of sitting where the double seats are in rows facing in the same direction. Each pair of seats has to fill up with single travellers or with determined couples before anyone will sit beside you. I always travel with my back to Dublin, letting Belfast fade away in front of me. That makes it even less likely that I will have anyone next to me. Most people, instinctively, hopefully, travel facing forwards. But on this Friday I have chosen to sit at a table with two double seats facing each other. I want to spread out.

As the train moves off a woman in her mid-sixties sits opposite me, sharing my table. She takes the aisle seat, so that we are at a respectful diagonal. We exchange 'hellos' of reassurance, and I go to my book, an intense Hungarian novel, all dialogue and a plot which is the fulfilment of a lifelong recrimination. It lasts me, at one reading breath, until well after Lisburn. Then I catch on the thorn of a sentence, a thing said by a character, which is too much for me, too close to my own intimacies, and I look up to watch the regular fields of mid-Down begin to change to the soaked land around Lurgan. She is reading a magazine. One that is scandal-ridden and astonished at the lifestyles of celebrities. Here are golfers, TV presenters, has-beens. The photo-shoots circulate around some man perched on the edge of a sofa with an arm around a wife. There are pastel v-neck jumpers and rooms which have gold and glass in the furniture.

We have made eye contact.

'It's a great train, all the same,' she says.

'Yes, it is.' And not wanting to leave it at that, since she has offered this, I add; 'It's very quick.'

'Two hours. Just two hours. Do you know I never was in Dublin in my life until last year? Well, except for my honeymoon. My daughter just moved there. I'm going to see her now.'

'That's nice.'

'She has lovely children. Two girls. Lovely children.'

'And will you stay for the weekend?'

'Oh yes. I'd stay and never come back if I could.' This is said with awful firmness. 'I would leave Northern Ireland behind once and for all if I could.' She closes the magazine and lays it face up on the table. She puts her hand on it, covering the eyes, but leaving exposed the laconic smile, of the Crown Prince of Denmark. 'But you can't leave things just like that, can you?'

'No. You can't.' And I add the nothingness of 'you can't leave places behind when you've lived your life there.'

'Do you live in Dublin?' There is joyous envy in her voice. She is still carried on the force of that wish to find a new life beside her daughter and grandchildren.

'Yes. I've been there a few years now. I used to work in Belfast and live in Dublin. I was never off this train.'

'And now you live in Dublin … Are you married?'

'Yes, I am. That's why I had to get a job in Dublin. Commuting's no life.' She is looking at the Crown Prince's perfect teeth.

A pause. It's my turn. She's wishing there was no silence. I'd like to go back to the story in Hungary – the two friends, long estranged, now old men, are about to meet for the first time in decades. Her fingers are moving slowly over the magazine cover. The palm of her hand stays still. The fingers draw upwards, the tips becoming perpendicular. I have to add something more.

'Is your husband …' The banality of what I was going to say was 'staying at home', but then the words began to change as I said them, so that I was on the verge of saying 'dead'. But I couldn't say that.

She ends the sentence for me. 'Divorced. We got divorced. We should never have married.'

There is wet land outside. The fields are flat. In this little plain between the drumlins the track runs alongside a straightened river. Maybe it's a canal. I'm almost sure it's a canal. People walk their dogs on the path alongside the water. Except, that is, after heavy rain, because then the waterway swarms out and over the fields, and hawthorn trees are marooned in still, temporary ponds, deep green with the submerged grass waving slowly under the surface.

She looks straight at me. 'Can I tell you?'

Yes, she can tell me.

'I married young. We all did in those days. I trained to be a typist and I was going to be a secretary. I liked typing. And shorthand, that was what I really loved. It was the happiest time of my life, in that college, with all the other girls. We were all so young and fresh and glamorous. I met him one night at a dance. The girls thought that every man who asked you to dance was going to be your husband. They said, "You'll know he's the one." And then when you came back over to them from the dancing they'd say, "Is he the one?" I didn't know if he was when I danced with him but he was very nice. He had dark hair, he was tall, nicely dressed. We all wanted a man with dark hair. He was quiet too, but that was fine. I wouldn't have known then what to talk about with a man.

'We went to dances for a few months. I got a job in a solicitor's office. I'd go into work every day, and it was like I was in a film. When he asked me to marry him I just said "yes". I didn't even think of saying "no", or "maybe", or whatever else you could say. Just "yes". Then he hardly mentioned getting married again after that. But that seemed natural too. It was left to the women, to my mother and his mother, to arrange it all.

'So we got married. We had our honeymoon in Dublin. In the North Star Hotel. It's just across the road from the train station. Four nights in that hotel and each night I'd go to sleep after listening to the last train leave for Belfast, and wake up hearing the milk train arrive early in the morning.

'We had a little house in North Belfast. It was quiet. Life was quiet. I gave up work and in those days, when you married, you stopped going to dances. That was just the way it was.

'So we started to have little parties in the house on Fridays. On this particular night I had a few drinks and went to bed. I left them all downstairs drinking and playing cards. And the next thing it was morning. The sun was lighting up the pattern on the curtains. I opened my eyes, that morning after the party and there was my husband, beside me, and beside him another man. Blondie I always call him. And the two of them, thinking I was asleep, they started touching each other. I feigned sleep. If I'd got out of the bed then Blondie would have seen me in God's finery.

'I didn't really know what was going on. I knew it was wrong. Wrong for a married man to be doing such things, you understand. After they were finished he gave Blondie money. I just lay there with my eyes closed until they'd gone. That was the last night I ever slept in a bed with my husband.'

It is darkening outside. We both look out the window, eastwards – the mountains in the distance, and beyond them the sea, leaching light from the undersides of the clouds.

'So you got divorced?'

'No, no. The divorce was only a few years ago. We lived together. Separate rooms. I visited his a few times. We endured each other because I wanted to have children. I needed something that was mine.'

The scrubby valleys are dusk grey and dark blue. House lights and street lights are becoming distinct. The window reflects the carriage back into itself and I can see that she is looking at me, so I turn back to her.

'Did you have good friends?'

'I couldn't have talked to my friends about that kind of thing. I was brought up very strict. I was Presbyterian, you know?'

I'm about to tell her that, yes, I know. But she doesn't need me to.

'I went to the Minister of our church. I couldn't find a word for it. I thought he might know what it was, that he might have some way to say it, but he never gifted me it. I just told him what had happened. About Blondie and the money. He looked at me like he was going to say something, then had me kneel down with him and say a prayer. Together we asked God for forgiveness. Then he stood up and said he was going to get his wife. I sat there and waited. They had one of those square mantelpiece clocks that people got then for wedding presents. Two holes on the face for winding it and a tick that would go through you. The room smelt of shortbread and books.

'In his wife came, and, do you know, she sat down and explained to me the facts of life. Youngster that I was, I was angry enough to give her cheek. I said to her, "That sounds great, I must try it some time." She cried. And I cried too. Her husband came back into the room when he heard the noise. He stood there looking at the two of us crying on the sofa. "What will I do?" I said to him. "What will I do?" "You'll live your life like a fetch," he said. That was all. I left him and I never went back to his church. Like a fetch. I rang my mother later to ask what it meant. I told her I'd overheard someone sitting behind me on the bus say it. She said she hadn't heard it for years. A country expression. "It means you'll be your own ghost."'

Soon we'll cross the border. After that the land will flatten out. The hedges and undulations of farmland will only just shield us from the sea, then this coyness will give way and we'll be alongside the coast, and the lights of the city will grow stronger, and the apartments, keeping their promises of privacy and of lives ready to be led, will turn their backs to the train.

Katherine Leyton

Body

We live in my lungs.
You smoke. I don't.
You set up an armchair in the corner,

bring your books and newspapers, lean back,
read and exclaim facts, something about the fall
of empires and the decline of women.

On the back of one of your magazines
a girl poses in a dress, straps
slipping down her shoulders,

something moving under her skin
as if it knew the place, something
I recognise like I recognise

the fire in my belly, burning
everything into threads of light,
sending smoke up through my eyes and mouth.

There is always another side to history.
In the factories where dress threads come together
the women hum to drown their hunger.

Art is a looking-glass.

I see myself in a painting, the one
in which the heroine's breasts are like bruised apples
and a shadow watches from the window.

When the girl in the photograph – or
the one in the painting, for that matter –
fucks, there is a heat that does not stop.

Forget flowers. Imagine instead
a throw of black, blue, green and gold,
each string unravelling.

What you meant – when you mentioned
the decline of women – was
that empires nearing

the brink of collapse
make stars out of women's eyes,
turn their bodies into metaphor.

Richard Gere's Grand Piano

Here, this is it:
you work as a waitress. You
bring people their French toast

and bacon. You can't pay the hydro bill.
I used to think of you as somebody

grand, like one of those pianos Gere
fucked Roberts on in *Pretty Woman*.

And that's the thing – maybe
 you are one of those pianos.

Maybe your greatest talent
is sparkling in empty foyers.

Advertisements

Narratives imagine God is Listening.
His Listening sounds like synthesized violins.

Certain nights I imagine God is a man
in a cardigan sweater, resting his hands
comfortably in pockets, winking at me

from the television, asking me what I'm
selling. I'm not sure. We watch a girl
at The Gap fold a sweater. I cup a breast

and measure my waist and ask God if
my sanity is like that sweater, collapsed
in a box with a ribbon around it. *Ahh,*

he says, *the girls in their Revlon!* And His
real soundtrack comes on – so catchy! –
and the cardigan comes off and begins to dance –

Allan Wilson

'How some can be good'
Extract from the novel *Meat*

Spaghetti was boiling in the pot. In the other one the mince was bubbling over and I lifted the lid to smell it. My Mum was stirring the spaghetti.

Don't give Annie any pasta, I said.

There's nothing to her, she said. I've made it now.

Give the extra to me then.

Annie had bought salad leaves and I got the packet out the fridge. I made a ring around the edge of a plate with the leaves.

I took my Mum by the shoulder. See if you stick the mince right in the middle there, it's like spaghetti, see? Just the rings of leaves there instead of the spaghetti.

Oh very clever of you, very artistic.

Annie was working through a pile of essays. I sat down and said she wasn't getting any pasta. I said, you're not getting any pasta, wee yin. Not allowed. Forbidden. What have you got to say about that? She rubbed my arm and went back to the essays. Then she dropped the pen.

We should go out tonight. I can do these tomorrow.

So it's a date you're after?

You want to go a drive somewhere?

I do want to go a drive. Or we could go a walk. I looked out the window. It's a bit chilly but at least it's dry. Eat one of your five a day then go a walk. Or we could go the pictures? To the pub? Pictures and the pub?

We spoke about going a walk. She wanted me to take her about and show her my old primary school again. She said, I want to see that bit where you used to play football. I want to take a photo of it on my phone. If it's still light then, deal? If not then we can go a drive or whatever. I said there was a football in my wardrobe and we could take it and play.

Maybe I should finish my work first though, she said. Should I? They'll all be asking me for what mark they got. Really I should be finishing these essays.

Does an extra day really matter? Will the kids not understand that your boyfriend had to take you on a date?

Dinner, my Mum called.

Annie's plate was hot. She put the cushion on her knees and I handed her the plate to rest it on top. In the kitchen my Mum was still dishing spaghetti for me. It was about three feet high on the plate. When she poured the bolognaise on it started pouring down the sides. I looked at her.

Do you think you've given me enough?

You said Annie didn't want any, so.

It was heavy. Had to use both hands then position it on the arm of the seat and attack the food from the bottom. I got an idea. I balanced the plate then ran through to the kitchen. I got a bowl from the cupboard and a wooden spoon from the pot. When I went back through I started taking spoonfuls from the big plate and putting them in the bowl. My Mum and Annie were watching.

Really? my Mum said. Talk about melodramatic.

I was careful with the moves. I only took small spoonfuls, kept the mince inside the lines. I was Alexander Walker. Meat was my friend. I knew how it operated and how it moved. But there was too much of it. Pieces were sliding down the spaghetti mound and I had to make a dam with the back of my fork to stop it sliding off the plate.

See? See the havoc you're causing? my Mum said.

I flipped the fork over and scooped some mince into my mouth. The hot sauce. I couldn't breathe. My tongue swelled up. I reached for my can. Empty. The spaghetti was becoming saturated with the sauce and was sinking into itself. It was hanging limp off the side of the plate. I scooped it back up but some strands slipped through the prongs of the fork, hit the arm of the couch then slid to the carpet.

My mouth's on fire.

Are you okay? Annie said.

You're making a mess, my Mum said.

Annie lifted her can and reached out to me. I kept one hand on my plate and drank quickly. She took the can back.

My Mum was on the other couch watching all this. Her plate was almost spaghetti free.

Have you given me your spaghetti as well? What is this? Why did you use the fiery sauce?

I eat too much, she said. You're a growing boy. She looked at Annie. Can you believe how he talks to his Mum?

Annie said tut tut tut and carried on with her dinner.

I managed to secure enough of the spaghetti in the bowl without any more spilling. I went to the kitchen and filled a pint glass with water. I ate quickly. When I'd polished off the bolognaise sauce there was still a plate full of spaghetti and more in the bowl. I tipped it on. There was some bolognaise sauce at the base. When it landed on spaghetti mountain it soaked into the pasta and disappeared. Annie got up and told my Mum dinner had been lovely. She carried her plate through to the kitchen. I heard her turning the taps on to wash them. My Mum looked across and smiled at me.

Just leave it if it's too much.

I twirled my fork and stuffed my face. I bit down hard on the strands until it became mush in my mouth.

When she came back Annie looked past me to watch the TV.

Where will we go a walk? I said.

Are yous going out? my Mum said. It's meant to freeze tonight.

A walk or a drive, Annie said.

I said we were going a walk. That I was insulated, had lined my stomach with the pasta, that if we got stranded I could just regurgitate and it'd come out still looking like spaghetti. Annie said to stop being so rank.

Just leave the rest, my Mum said.

I was starting to make a dent in it. If I left it she'd hold it against me. I pay for your meals and you don't even eat them. I go out of my way to cook for you and you don't even finish it. Is my food not good enough for you two? You can make your own food if that's how you feel. I looked at her and shoved another mouthful in. I could feel my insides starting to seize up. I put a hand on my stomach and it felt like prodding a brick. I drank more of the water. When it mixed with the pasta in my mouth it felt like each strand was soaking it up and getting fatter. I chewed and bit.

Are you okay? Annie said.

Leave it God sake, my Mum said.

Or take a break at least, Annie said.

My Mum came over and went to take the plate. I grabbed the other side and held on tight.

Why didn't you get me to bring in mince? I said.

Here we go, she said.

This stuff is inferior. I knew the minute I tasted it. You can't hide it Mum. It's not even like my stuff's more expensive. Not with the staff discount.

There's no difference.

No difference! Seriously? Right well is this lean steak mince or just steak mince?

Lean.

Naw it isn't!

I'm sure it is.

Show us the packet then.

I've binned it.

Well I'll get it out then. I went to stand up. Do you want me to? Can you not just tell me the truth and say that you got the steak mince instead of the lean steak mince.

They're both the same anyway, she said.

Ahh! Admits it! This stuff is full of fat, Mum. And Annie's on a diet as well.

You're not funny, Annie said.

Well you are. She is. I'm just saying, if you're needing mince then I'll bring it in. I'll even pay for it. Honestly. There's no point getting this stuff, it's just garbage. I'm just saying. I'm happy to get the good stuff for you. It's not that I don't appreciate it, you know. Annie and my Mum looked at each other. Naw, I do. I don't know. Seriously. It's nice, it's just, I'm saying I can get you the better stuff. It's not a problem.

Just leave it if you're not wanting it, she said.

My fork dropped. It bounced on the spaghetti like a cushion and settled in. I inhaled as much air as I could.

I'll have a break, I said.

They went back to watching the TV. I could feel my pulse beating in my temple. My skin felt tight all over. I knew if I stretched my eyes would pop out. I turned to Annie. Why do you think Chekhov never wrote stories about snooker players?

She shrugged. Maybe he did. He wrote a lot of stories.

He should have written about snooker players. I bet he did. Maybe he wrote about someone in a supermarket. He wrote about a teacher.

They won't have had supermarkets back then.

You should write a story about me, I said.

My Mum made a noise through her lips then started to laugh.

Wait until you've won the world championships, she said. That would be a story.

What about you? Annie said.

Just how I play snooker. About the guys in the club.

That's daft, my Mum said.

She was staring across at me. I cracked my neck from side to side and lifted my fork.

Stop being stubborn and leave it. If it's too much for you to finish then just go and scrape it into the bin.

You should get one of those measuring rings, Annie said. Have you seen them?

No, I don't … what is it?

It's this ring where you have a lever and you can turn it depending how many people are eating the spaghetti. If it's one portion the ring opens only so much that you can fit that amount of spaghetti in. If you set it to two portions then it'll fit more and so on.

They carried on speaking but I focused on the food. I chewed slowly. My jeans tightened around my thighs. I wanted to get a pair of scissors and slice up my legs. I imagined my legs being like spaghetti, when I cut the jeans open it would splay out across the room. Strands stuck into my socks. I heard pieces of their conversation, words and phrases, great invention, he'll be a millionaire, I'll pick you one up, revolutionise cooking, we're on diets anyway. It got that there was only a forkful left. I looked at the two of them and grinned.

You'll need to brush your teeth, Annie said.

Well done, my Mum said.

I can't believe you ate all that.

I'm Mr Spaghetti, I said.

The fork was piled high and I put it in my mouth. It was the best mouthful I'd had. The texture was so soft against my teeth. I wanted to die eating spaghetti. I wanted to eat it every day for the rest of my life. Beds should be stuffed with it. Pillows padded on the inside with cooked spaghetti. I wanted to tell my Mum that maybe she was half Italian, maybe she should be cooking on TV, showing them how it's done.

Thanks for dinner, I said.

Did you enjoy it?

Annie giggled.

The best dinner I've ever had, I said. No question about it. It filled a gap.

More pasta if you want it tomorrow, my Mum said.

Annie groaned and covered her eyes.

If that's what you want to cook, I said.

Oh I'll cook whatever you two feel like, my Mum said.

Well please then, more spaghetti. I'm a growing boy.

I'll give you mine and Annie's too then. Sound good?

Great. Thanks.

I stood up to carry the plate and the bowl through. The pains came back. Things dislodged other things inside me. When I moved my arms I got a pain in my head. I felt my jaw ache when I shifted my leg. At one point Annie poked me in the belly and said she'd cook soon. She said she'd got this South Beach recipe from Lynne in her work. She said Lynne was forty but her body was in great shape. She ran a 5k every night.

If I only had a spare five hours every night, my Mum said.

I think it takes her thirty minutes, Annie said.

That's what I mean, my Mum said. Half an hour for her, five hours for me.

We could go running together, Annie said.

This body wasn't built for running, my Mum said.

It wasn't built for cooking either, I said.

The two of them looked at me.

Excuse me? my Mum said. Can you believe he says that about his Mum?

Sexist, Annie said.

I went back through to the kitchen and shouted that I'd do the dishes. It relaxes me. Frees up the mind to think about other things. I said that if I could get a job washing dishes, listening to music all day I'd be happy. My Mum came through. There was some spaghetti still in the pot. I reached in and plucked a strand out. She was watching me. I let it hover above my mouth then dropped it in.

Do you want me to make some more? If you're still hungry?

Nah, I'll maybe grab something from the chippy when we're out. Maybe get a curry or something. Doner kebab.

So that's what you call quality meat?

Doner isn't too bad actually. Just it's got lots of water.

I turned the tap on to do the dishes but she squeezed in and lifted the sponge.

If you wash I'll dry, I said.

There's not enough room.

You go and sit down then, I'll do them.

Away you go.

I like it but.

Wheesht. Go away your walk. Away and look after your girlfriend. She shouted through to Annie. I'm saying he has to look after you and leave these dishes.

I'll live, Annie said.

Away you go. If yous are going out go now before it's too cold.

I went through and stood against the living room wall. I rested on the radiator and used it to keep me up. The heat was going through my jeans and the skin was starting to nip. I felt the heat going down my legs, up my back.

Will we go a walk or a drive? Annie said.

I don't mind.

She came over and stood beside me.

I think maybe we should just stay in, she said. You look done in.

I'm fine, I said.

I can see that. She prodded my stomach again. It's just for me. I want to stay in. We should watch a film. I'll finish marking my essays.

And what will I do?

You look like you could do with a sleep.

I'll read, I said.

Upstairs I locked the door. Annie was setting up piles on the bed and I lay down beside her.

We need to get our own place, I said.

We will.

She's gonna end up killing me. Did you have that sauce?

I'm okay with spicy stuff.

She did it on purpose. She's after my blood. Must think I've got life insurance or something.

There'd be easier ways to do it than with hot sauce.

Like what?

She could stab you. Accidentally on purpose.

She wouldn't stab her own son.

Yeah, but she could. If she wanted to. While you were asleep. We could wake up in the middle of the night with her standing over us, a kitchen knife in her hand.

Lightning flashing in the window, crazy look in her eye, aye, I see it now. That would be easier than hot sauce.

See?

I jumped on the bed beside her and got my book from the drawer.

You sure you don't want to go out?

Maybe after I've marked these. What shift are you tomorrow? Seven four or eight five?

Seven four.

You can take the car cos I'm out.

I might go and get a game of snooker.

Good idea. Keep up the practising then win that tournament.

It's in the bag. We should just book a holiday now.

I opened the book and she began to mark. It was the shortest story in the book. It's a cold night in Russia and a student's going home after a day out hunting. He doesn't like how cold and dark it is. He's starving, miles from home. He thinks how a thousand years ago people would have been as cold and hungry. He thinks they still will in another thousand years. He's down in the dumps. There were miserable people always. It'd never get better. He doesn't want to go home.

He goes up to an allotment and sees people he knows around a bonfire. The women are washing pots and plates. He speaks with an old woman and warms himself by the fire. He starts telling her that Peter the Apostle warmed himself by a fire once. Then he tells her about the Last Supper. How Peter said to Jesus that he'd back him up, follow him to prison or death or anywhere. And how Jesus says to Peter that by the time the cock crows twice he'll have denied him three times. The student keeps telling the old woman this story. He says how Peter couldn't sleep cos he was so worried about what Jesus had said. And when Judas betrayed him and Jesus was taken, Peter followed his mate. At some point Peter stands around a fire and a woman spots him and says, that guy should be taken and questioned too, he was Jesus's disciple.

The student tells the old woman that it happened when Peter was warming himself by a fire just like the one they're standing around. He says that when the crowd started asking Peter if he knew Jesus, Peter said he'd never met the guy. Later on another person says, here, that guy was always with Jesus. But once again Peter says he never knew Jesus. It happens again. He denies everything. And then the cock crows. The student tells this story to the old woman as they stand around the fire. He looks into the flames and tells her that when Peter realised what he'd done he went to the garden and cried.

The old woman has to look away from the fire. She has to wipe her eyes with her sleeve as if she's embarrassed.

The men who work in the allotment return from the river. The student says goodbye to the old woman and starts walking again. He notices the dark and the cold again. He feels freezing. But he begins to think of the old woman and he wonders why the story of Peter meant what it did to her. He thinks that even though it was nineteen centuries before, the story still had meaning. That he was the same as her and they were both the same as Peter. He begins to feel happy.

He carries on home. He sees his village. And he thinks that the most important things in the world are truth and beauty. He feels young. He feels happy but doesn't know why.

I didn't get the story so I read it again. It made me smile because I was the same age as the student. I thought it was about moments. How some can be good. I looked at Annie. I ran my hand through her hair. Fifteen to go, she said. I sat back on the bed. It was getting dark. The sun had broken through but now it was disappearing again. I could see the last of it in the reflection off the neighbours' windows.

Later I felt her kissing me. I'm finished, she said. I asked her what the time was and she showed me on her phone. I had to screw my eyes up from the brightness.

Will we go out? I said.

Are you hungry?

Aye, fuckin starving!

You're cozy, she said.

She lifted the covers and climbed in beside me.

We'll go out another night, she said.

It was dark outside. She reached out the bed to get the lamp and I felt a chill come in. But when she came back it got nice just as fast. I closed my eyes again. She was sleeping first. I felt her breathing get steady. I checked the alarm. Annie had set it for me. I couldn't remember dreaming. I closed my eyes. Snooker. I saw the balls falling into the pockets. The table clearing quickly. I was building breaks. Red, black, red, black. Then the table was full again. I kept potting but the table never cleared. I opened my eyes and pulled the covers tight around me. I felt for Annie's hand and held it.

Ron Butlin

Dancing in Princes Street

First Dance (Scottish Country Dancing)

A clown in face-paint, kilt and trainers. Bagpipes.
Standing legs apart to blow strathspeys and reels
the full length of Princes Street while clowns and fairies
heel-and-toe the stationary afternoon, strip-the-willow
between deserted traffic islands and summer-yellow
windowless police vans. Fluttering their paper wings. Sunlight,
on their stardust skin.
Handclapped time comes shuddering back
from boarded-up shop windows, steel-barricaded shop doors.
Laughter's shredded by helicopter blades.

Meanwhile, the likes of you and me look on, penned in
behind the RSA pillars for our comfort and security.
So many wallflowers at the dance.

Second Dance (Slow)

Leaving Stockbridge at three a.m., grabbing the after-hours funicular
that runs from Lyell and Catherine's up to George Street,
the Mound, The Meadows and home.
Halfway there, the Rioja running out on us, our effortlessly upwards glide
jams, shudders. Gears lock. Traction slips, and one of us nearly
hits the cobbles …

A few stumble-steps later we spread our wings.

Soaring high above Princes Street, gliding north,
south, east and west –

Following the unseen ley-lines of our city and the unspoken certainties
of our heart, we'll never fear a fall to earth.

Third Dance (Hokey-cokey)

Time for the formal ball, invitation only.

Dress code: fluorescent orange and hard hats. Health & Safety boots.
Clipboards for the dance cards.

The first band strikes up –

The second band strikes up –

The third band strikes up –

One, Two, Three and –

You dig a big hole here, you dig a big hole there,
You dig the biggest hole ever and another as a spare.
You shut the city down, take a six-month break
& that's what it's all about!

Hey!

You plan a tram route up, you plan a tram route down,
You plan another plan for the centre of the town,
You rip the new line out and you start it all again
& that's what it's all about!

Hey!

The Last Dance

The first black wall moves closer. Then the second. The third.

The woman PC's so young she needs only pigtails and a brace
to look her real age. What music did she hear back in Primary –
saying *Yes* when asked to dance the black-walled dance,
saying *No* to stardust and wings?

She strolls over to the wallflowers –
Careful, sir – my colleagues will be moving in soon.

Meanwhile the black visors, body armour, shields, batons, boots.
What music will *they* dance to? What steps
have *they* learned?

David Hume Takes a Last Walk on Arthur's Seat

Not bothering to set his alarm clock David Hume
took to his deathbed. He lay down, got himself comfortable and closed his eyes.
On this most special occasion, he pictured a real summer's afternoon
smelling of heather, sun-warmed rocks,
a hint of sea-air blowing in from the Forth.
At peace, he let the grass and whins of Arthur's Seat come sloping down
to welcome him.

Just then an untidy-looking sheep glanced up, interrupting
its day-long meal. It stared at him.
What happens now? asked the dying man. The sheep stood its ground,
blinked. Stopped chewing.
Well? prompted the sceptic's sceptic, whose studies had reinforced
his belief that in such matters we each need
all the help we can get.

Well? Well?

The lightly sketched-in clouds were stationary. The sun stood still
for the first time since that ancient god had stopped it briefly
in its tracks, in the name of love.

The sheep strolled over. It coughed, and was about to speak when –

Visitors. Bloody visitors. Hume could hear them barging in through his front door,
cluttering up his hallway with their endless taking off of hats and wigs,
their loud disrobing of noisy raincoats, their pulling off
of sopping-wet summer galoshes.
Their standing around discussing him in whispers.

Meanwhile his perfect afternoon was heading nowhere –
the sheep had thinned down to a dwindling hank of scrag-wool on sticks;
the clouds condensing into raindrops that would never fall;
the hillside's green and broom-yellow dissolving into
ever-weakening sunlight.
Here and there, his bedroom furniture was already showing through.

Uninvited callers! Comforting words! Concern for his mortal soul!

He fights back. Eyes firmly closed to blot out this micro-flock
of ministers determined on his salvation,
Hume returns to Arthur's Seat. He repositions the sun
and sets it moving across the sky once more,
he restores the nearest clouds as best he can,
fills in enough of the path to let him walk in safety.

Come nightfall, he's reached the summit. Edinburgh lies spread out
far below.

He takes his first step into utter and perpetual darkness –
and the darkness holds.

Another step. And then another.

Soon he's walking directly above the city. Unnamed stars and
undiscovered galaxies congregate around him.
He knows each step could be his last. *As in life,*
he whispers, *so let it be in death.*

And smiling to himself alone, he puts his best foot forward.

Tony McKibbin

The Spiritually Ravenous
Why *We Need to Talk About Kevin*

Lynne Ramsay used to be not only the great hope for British cinema but the great Scottish hope too. And Ramsay is a woman. How many British let alone Scottish filmmakers were there who were offering a feminised perspective in cinema? There have of course been important British female directors, from theorist Laura Mulvey to Scotland's own brilliant minimalist Margaret Tait, Sally Potter to Andrea Arnold – but when Ramsay got lost in production hell working on an Alice Sebold adaptation *The Lovely Bones*, it looked like Hollywood had another victim: another filmmaker who died, in critic Pauline Kael's words, in the only place where you can die of encouragement. However, Ramsay has returned, adapting another hit novel to the screen. Ramsay might not have been making films during the near decade between *Morvern Callar* and *We Need to Talk About Kevin*, but it is as though the fascination with a certain ethos continued percolating.

Though Lionel Shriver's book became a topic of much discussion around the issue of good parenting and the problem of nature and nurture, Ramsay's adaptation focuses (like her earlier *Ratcatcher* and *Morvern Callar*) on a different question. What is it to possess moral, even spiritual consciousness after the event, and especially when that event happens to involve the death of others? *Ratcatcher* begins with the death of Jamie's friend Brian after they've been playing in a canal. In *Morvern Callar*, the titular character takes off after her boyfriend's death rather than immediately informing the police. In *We Need to Talk About Kevin*, we gradually come to understand that Eva (Tilda Swinton) is ostracised by the community in which she still lives because of her son Kevin's high school killing spree. Is she, like Jamie and Morvern, also a culpable character, someone whom we might feel is partly responsible for her son's deeds? As the film slowly and elliptically pieces the events together, so we muse over two moral arcs at work. There is Kevin's possibly burgeoning awareness of the enormity of his deeds, but also the sense that Eva might not be the entirely blameless mother.

It is Kevin's hint of redemption that gives the film its heft, but it is Eva's perspective that gives the film its form in its concern with Kevin's evolution from young child, to spree-killer, to someone with a smidgen of self-reflection in the face of atrocity; all seen from the mother's frustrated point of view.

In Ramsay's films there is a fragmentary dimension; it is as if the social world is less important than the private one but it is one where there are still social imperatives as ethical choices. If in each film the social imperative is of willing that your action be universally applicable, then the youthful characters fail. Two question overcomes them like a moral backwash. Has what they have done unto others lacked moral awareness? And how does such an awareness come about?

Jamie is a twelve-year-old boy, Morvern a young adult, and we see Kevin from birth through to his late teens. Their level of culpability is far from equivalent. Jamie seems to have drowned his friend accidentally; Morvern simply doesn't report her boyfriend's death; whereas Kevin commits mass murder. However, Ramsay's approach to the problem of responsibility is consistent. It is as if she wants to obliterate ready causal relations to search out tenuous ones. Her achievement in *We Need to Talk About Kevin* is not to create an issue film, but instead to offer up a sensual exploration of the inexplicable, where the purpose is more associational rather than causal – closer, in Jean Piaget's terms, to 'the child's conception of the world', over that of the adult. Piaget reached the conclusion in the book of that title that 'logic develops as thought becomes socialised', adding, 'So long as the child supposes that everyone necessarily thinks like himself, he will not spontaneously seek to convince others, nor to accept common truths, nor, above all, to prove or test his opinions.' Out of socialising and such reason, can come cause and effect, but Ramsay is wary of such causal development. 'I'm very interested in focusing on details and making audiences see things they don't normally see,' she says in *Sight and Sound* (October 1999). 'What I do a lot in *Ratcatcher* is frame something so that it's what you don't see that's important.'

Ramsay has said that *We Need to Talk About Kevin* is conceived so much from Eva's point of view, that she would like to make two more films from the story – from the points of view of the father, Franklin, (John C. Reilly) and Kevin (Ezra Miller). Yet if what we don't see is of such importance, then don't we have these other perspectives anyway? A film from Kevin's angle might be a little too close to an *expression* of character, might indicate reasons and motives that Ramsay would prefer to keep tentative.

Being from Eva's perspective allows the film both to create mystery and to extend culpability. We see Kevin not as a demon child sent from hell but a child born of a reluctant mother who expresses her doubts about having a child at the very moment of conception. She looks uneasy throughout her despondent pregnancy and even as she is giving birth she seems reluctant to let Kevin enter the world. The nature of her experience as a new mother is encapsulated in the scene when she finds the sound of his crying so unbearable that she seeks relief by standing next to a construction worker jackhammering in the street: a sound loud enough to drown out the wailing of her distressed infant.

When her husband suggests moving out of New York and up to Connecticut, Eva is reluctant to forgo city living. Franklin tells her it would be best for Kevin and they make the move. As if seeking to reconnect with her former identity as a travel writer, she decorates her study according to her own preoccupation: with maps. Like a prison lifer protesting with his own waste, Kevin promptly covers the walls with paint from a paint-gun, the results curiously resembling a Jackson Pollack. Eva is plunged into such despair it is as if she truly wishes Kevin had never been born.

In refraining from presenting such moments from within Kevin's consciousness, Ramsay ensures that it is Kevin who remains mysterious. His motives and potential for violence are a matters of tense concern, but hold their ambiguity until the very end. It is partly because we are privy to Eva perspective and not Kevin's that we may withhold final judgement, no matter the horror of his deeds.

Ramsay's fascination with the detrital over the tidy, the chaotic over the organised is in evidence both in form and content. Albeit the film is seen from Eva's angle, we might wonder whether the mise-en-scene – the film's staging – hints at Kevin's; for example, the opening scene of a tomato harvest parade in Spain, which shows Eva splattered with red juice, borne aloft amid a swarm of bodies, in an state of messy bliss.

Kevin's determination to rebel is manifested in a moment where just after his nappy has been changed he forces another bowel movement into his new one. It is an act of defiance Eva meets with an act of violence, throwing him against a wall as if succumbing to Kevin's messy feelings instead of asserting her own rational behaviour.

Eva and Franklin may have moved to Connecticut 'for Kevin', but the arid, roomy house looks more suitable as a yoga retreat than for bringing up a boy who possesses some of the character traits of Damien in the *Omen*. Every fault and flaw in the mother–son relationship seems to be taking place in an echo chamber. Rather than being a tranquil space, it feels so uselessly empty it demands something messy to counter the sterile environment. 'That mansion house was so creepy,' Ramsay told *Sight and Sound* (November, 2011). 'There are so many of those follies out there, especially in Connecticut. I talked to the designers a lot about making it seem like a set, even though it wasn't a set – because everything is becoming a performance within their family.'

It is as though Kevin tries to create as much chaos as he can to counter the sterile environment, and logically extends it to the school.

In choosing to shoot in a wide-screen format that plays up the width and turns a domestic story into an epic battle, Ramsay seems half on the side of Kevin's need to violate the environment, to turn the milieu into the fragile over the strong, the chaotic over the neat; yet well aware, also, that Kevin's actions are often manipulation writ large. This is Oedipal hell as power game: Kevin doesn't want to sleep with his mother and kill his father, so much as to masturbate in front of her (she catches him in the bathroom), and kill the father and sister as if in a final act of one-upmanship over Eva.

Ramsay's interest in chaos deriving from a fragility of perspective taken further here than in *Ratcatcher* and *Morvern Callar* – into the very form. Her first two films capture the snatched moments without the full perspective. Brian's death in *Ratcatcher* is elliptically presented, and through the partial framing of many of the characters we appear to be caught in the middle of a perception, not fully aware of the whole scene. Frequently Ramsay shows us a midriff, a foot, a hand, a part of the body that would seem incidental rather than central. As she says in relation to one scene: 'The close-up of Margaret Anne's knee reminds people of childhood, but it also says something about her character as well. From that tiny little detail, that close-up of her body, I think you understand that she's a bit brutalised herself.' (*Sight and Sound*, October 1999) However, the use of the elliptical to suggest the whole is integral to the editing of *We Need to Talk About Kevin*; and it allows Ramsay to stay consistent with her fascination with the body from a sensitised angle.

The film offers snatches of scenes and the big set-piece is all but eschewed for its repercussive effects. Rather than detailing the massacre, Ramsay instead uses it for its emotional *effect* as opposed to its adrenalised *impact*. When Geoff King in *New Hollywood Cinema* and elsewhere talks of impact aesthetics, he does so to emphasise partly the fascination with the set-piece, evident, for example, in *Mission Impossible*, 'which includes numerous sequences of high tension and or/explosive action but climaxes with an outlandish set-piece involving a helicopter chasing a train into the Channel Tunnel'. In such films, the sequence as impact is far more important than any bodily and emotional damage done to the characters. Ramsay, on the other hand, looks for repercussive impact. We often get glimpses of the massacre after a moment of emotional pain, as in the scene where a couple of women walk along the street and one of them slaps Eva, and the action momentarily flashes back to hint at the context for the slap; later, a young man in a wheelchair speaks sympathetically to her and it's revealed, in similar fashion, that he is a victim of the massacre.

Numerous filmmakers go down the impact aesthetic route, turning the body into an arena of spectacle as people are blown to pieces in vast numbers – like software to the dominant hardware of planes, trains and automobiles. Along with a handful of other international filmmakers, including Andrea Arnold, Lucrecia Martel and Angela Shanelec, Ramsay is more interested in the repercussive impact, in the human software. It is partly why she invokes the fragile and chaotic, undermines the hardness of things, the robust absence of feeling.

But if after-effect is more important than impact, then of course moral delay in Ramsay's work is of more importance than pragmatic, ethical decision-making. If Ramsay removes the set-piece, she also removes moral co-ordinates. *We Need to Talk About Kevin* is nothing if not a film about culpability rather than morality, about the subtlety of emotional responsibility rather than the broad ethical vistas that make actions so clearly right and wrong. The implicit question is: where here does blame lie, with the person committing the deeds, or with the parents who may be held responsible for creating a child's moral compass? Certainly others in her community feel Eva is responsible. But does the film itself impute guilt through a narrative structure that deliberately refuses to create a broader social context for Kevin's actions than the Oedipal struggle with mum? While Kevin says he doesn't much care for friends (and there is indeed no evidence of them), Ramsay could easily have given us the school context that leads up to the murders. It is as though in this film she consciously decides to invert the socio-logic of the school environment of *Elephant,* Gus Van Sant's account of a high school massacre; and to focus on the psycho-logical in concentrating on subconscious resentment on Eva's part and burgeoning resentment on Kevin's.

In the scene where Kevin defecates in his nappy and Eva throws him against the wall, he is shown as a little boy who knows that power and bullying work, and also who has a sense that his mother is finally letting out her true feelings towards him. Here, the film resembles a chamber piece where two characters play power games and negotiate for control; *The Offence, Garde à vue, Sleuth, A Simple Formality, Death and the Maiden* come to mind. However, in this instance conditioning coincides with the conditional; it is as if Kevin intuits that Eva has never given unconditional love – and, consequently, there is something askew in the conditioning process.

Some will insist Ramsay's film defies a psychological reading, but therein lie two dangers. One is to reduce Kevin to a stock character from a horror film – where, as Donald Pleasence says of young Michael Myers in *Hallowe'en*, a character is 'pure evil'. The other is to ignore Ramsay's interest in ethos, in watching how people *behave*. Whether it is the cruelty of the kids in *Ratcatcher*, or the insensitivity of the adults by the swimming pool at the Spanish holiday resort in *Morvern Callar*, Ramsay searches out *dynamics*. In response to people wondering whether Kevin is a two-dimensional personification of evil, Ramsay says in a *Time Out* interview, 'the only time you see him behave like that is with her [his mother]'. The suggestiveness resides in showing Kevin as a bad seed, but locally so: an identity shaped by circumstances too narrow. If Kevin is malicious around his mother, and spends most of his time around her, how much of his personality then becomes malicious? It is as though Kevin doesn't *trust* his mother's affection, as if he senses that she yearns for a life very different from the one she has looking after him.

But of course, come the end of the film, we find out that Eva has no one in her life any longer – except Kevin – and that she can find no work other than at a shoddy travel agent. If childbearing denied her the career arc she might have hoped for, then the road she ends on is the road to hell – this is a comment she actually makes when a couple of Mormons tap on the door of her bungalow long after the killings. They asks where she thinks she is going to spend the afterlife. She replies she knows exactly where she'll be going: straight to hell.

Ramsay acknowledges her admiration for the great French filmmaker of the spiritual, Robert Bresson. In an *Observer* interview in November 2011, she states that his *Notes on the Cinematographer* remains a book of 'abiding importance'. Bresson's *Pickpocket* was inspired by Dostoyevsky's *Crime and Punishment*, in which the central character finds a hint of redemption in the love of a good woman, and there is something in Ramsay's discourse that suggests she is interested not so much in the nature/nurture debate, but in an ethical enquiry into the nature of love. It is as though Kevin has sought her unconditional love through a heinous act, and that the mother and son alike are part of an evil greater than either of them individually. That this is an evil brought about by the dynamic between them is invoked in Ramsay's comment about seeing Kevin chiefly within the context of Eva and the manner in which Eva becomes Kevin, and Kevin, Eva. Shortly before the end of the film Eva paints the bedroom in her humble abode the dark blue of Kevin's room, and it's as though in this space that so resembles her son's own private space before perpetrating the massacre, she is somehow taking responsibility for these actions, the doings of the child from her womb.

In *Ratcatcher* the ethical question seems to lead Jamie towards a likely demise in the canal where his friend died. In *Morvern Callar*, Morvern walks through the film as if in a daze, at one moment accepting her dead boyfriend's book as her own and travelling with the money as though in a paradoxical search for her soul: it takes an act of betrayal to possess the wherewithal to find herself, as she assumes the creative identity of someone else. In each instance, though, the characters remain within the realm of 'good'.

Kevin more obviously occupies the place of evil, and so the task of creating redemptive space is minimal, and for much of the film there is little in Ramsay's framing that indicates sympathy. As a toddler he is sullen and resentful; as a late teenager he is narcissistic and abrasive, a figure searching out man's lowest common denominator, and assuming it passes for the truth. There is the moment mentioned earlier where Kevin masturbates in the bathroom and continues deliberately when his mother catches him in the act. In another scene, Eva puts a disc of Kevin's into her computer and various porno images come up on screen and destroy her system. As opposed to Jamie and Morvern, who are circumstantially bad characters, Kevin's accumulation of bad deeds, and his relish towards them, makes him more obviously evil.

Can such evil be dispelled? And if comes out of the toxic dynamic of a mother and son, an Oedipal tragedy that has nothing to do with Sophocles, can it be turned around? If this is the implication of *We Need to Talk About Kevin*, can it, like *Ratcatcher* and *Morvern Callar*, be viewed as an ethical rite of passage film? Quite a demand, but this question appears to be part of the film's provocatively moral coda. There is an interesting, almost throwaway, passage in the book that Ramsay makes the very core of the film: 'Kevin seemed to want practically nothing. I now realise that he was spiritually ravenous.'

As Eva visits her son in jail yet again, presumably expecting that as in the previous two years he will sit in silence, suddenly, he talks – and gives the impression that maybe, somewhere, he recognis almost like a throwaway es the terrible nature of his deeds, and also possesses feelings for the woman who gave birth to him and who now stands by him. According to Sean O'Hagan's interview for the *Observer*:

> Ramsay auditioned nearly 500 teenage boys for the role,' many of whom, she says, 'instinctively got it, often disturbingly so'. In the end, Miller was cast because of how well he played the film's final scene, the one in which his teenage vulnerability and aloneness are glimpsed in a single glance between him and his mother.

It is of course too late to bring anybody back from the dead, except for one person: the titular character, who hints at his own moral resurrection. One thinks here of St Augustine's famous comment: 'The measure of love is to love without measure.' Even more pertinent is a fascinating, difficult remark from the moral philosopher Emmanuel Levinas in *Entre Nous*:

> Goodness, a childish virtue; but already charity and mercy and responsibility for the other, and already the possibility of sacrifice in which the humanity of man bursts forth, disrupting the general economy of the real and standing in sharp contrast with the perseverance of entities persisting in their being.

Perhaps few characters in film have persisted in their being quite to the detriment of others as does Kevin. But is there not a hint at the close that this persistence is beginning to waver as mother and son hug in a gesture that feels, for the first time, like an act of unconditional love on both their parts? This is the final question posed as with this film Ramsay continues to enquire into the nature not of nurture but of broader, deeper questions of the culpable.

Sean O'Brien

Lock-In

1

The oiled-up model in the garage calendar
Slipped off that bonnet a long time back.
Married and divorced a time or two
She has invested in a café bar
As far from here as she can get.
South Shields, perhaps. Rodrigues. Reunion.
Somewhere your sort haven't fucked up yet.
You wonder what she actually deserved
When she let fall her pleasant guise, her thin array.
The jukebox mutters *Let's Get Wet.*
She has to bear the light of scrutiny
Forever or until they tear it down,
Whichever is the longer, fading a little
As they say they do, paler and further
As the years go by, as quick quick slow
As replays of *Amore*. Time to go,
But no one moves, since no one
Wants to miss the spirit draw
Or the Exotic who has commandeered
The Ladies. Hypocrite buveurs!

2

There's been a funeral in the lounge
All day, the dead off the estate
Assembled to receive their own
With rich recrimination. You though
With your lives before you seem the last
To realise what's what, what's best,
To tell the signs from mere surroundings,
The figure from the ground, or if indeed
All this is only more periphrasis
Designed to tap a stranger, take the piss,
Or whether all these accidents are clues
To what there is when once you reach
The furthest annexe of the booze,
The Bower of Bliss and /or the Harpies' nest.

3

You say you're only stopping for the one.
Come in and let the great world pass you by,
That figment all the regulars deny.
The tarred interior, the years,
The air of practised discontent
And simultaneous too late / not yet,
All passion, plus the wages, spent
And bound to end in tears:
No need to wonder where they went –
Where else except in here
Whose ectoplasmic smoke and sweat

Alone appear to pay the rent?
In certain lights – a diving bell of malt,
A vodka tilting over the abyss of stout –
It has the flattering look of fate.
Eventually this is the place
That makes you long for ignorance again,
The one dim first-night room
An everywhere, a treasure-cave of alibis
And home to forty thieves
And their transactions: *blue pills, mek yer*
Spill yer muck all night, which leaves
Precisely nothing to be said, and all
Eternity to say it to the dead.

The Crimson Avenger

People are always not reading. It's too bloody hot.
It's too late for all that. It's too hard
Or not true or too long or too short or they're pissed.

Off like a shot at the drop of page seven.
But it's next on the list, or it would be.
It's not *Gnomes and Hardons*. Now that's good –

There's plenty to look at, for instance the gnomes.
But this horrible cover? The paper smells funny?
It's Thursday. Or Tuesday. It's Pentecost.

Something came up. Fuck me, it's in French.
It's horses for courses. Why only this morning
Somebody'd only just sat down to read

When in through the window who should arrive
But a Crimson Avenger intent on avenging
And waving his golden bazooka? You with me?

Try reading with that going on. You what?
Does the Crimson Avenger like reading?
He would, but it's finding the time.

Anneliese Mackintosh

Doctors

Congratulations and hurray for you!

What you have achieved is no mean feat. It makes you kind of special. Heroic, even. Not only did you get your Masters, you wee genius, but you got a Distinction. That's right; with a capital 'D'. You can put M.Litt. at the end of your name now, if you want to. You can show off about this for the rest of your life.

Thank goodness you didn't go to Paris to become a mime artist, like you said you would. Christ no, that Masters was definitely the right choice.

And by golly, you learnt so damn much. What did you learn again? You learnt that writing doesn't have to be like a million fireworks all going off at once. You learnt that you shouldn't try to illustrate your own work. You learnt that you have a distinctive and original voice. You learnt that having lunch with famous authors is overrated. And you learnt that it is possible to lose a condom inside yourself during a one night stand, only to find it two days later while doing a wee, oh horror, oh horror.

So what did you do after your Masters then, you whiz kid, you? Did you pen your great novel? Move abroad? Teach poor, sick children how to read and write? No, you did not. You took a full-time job in a card shop. At the card shop, you had to polish the front of every card in the shop, every morning.

After a week and a half, you began to miss uni. You were treated like a god at uni. You had lunch with Margaret Atwood at uni. You were never asked to polish the cards or count the novelty pencils at uni.

So on your day off you went back. Standing in the English Literature office, you told the course convenor you might like to do a PhD. When he asked why, you didn't mention Margaret Atwood or novelty pencils. You said: 'Because I want to be a Doctor, like my dad.' 'Okay,' he replied, 'that's as good a reason as any.' He handed you a thirty page application form with seventy-two pages of guidance notes, and then you polished cards and waited.

Sometime in late August, you received a letter saying your application had been successful. You were going to do a PhD. And what's more, you were going to be paid to do it.

The people at the card shop gave you an aloe vera plant when you left.

At this point you began to realise that you had no idea what a PhD actually was. All you knew was that your dad had one, in Electronic Engineering, and his had gone so well he went to America and met Bill Gates. Oh, and you had also seen PhD students around campus and knew what they looked like. So you bought yourself a few cardigans, to fit in, and practised your lunch conversation with Bill Gates, just in case.

*

So here you are now, you clever thing, sitting in your flat with a load of cardigans and an empty computer screen. What are you going to do first? Well, before you can write anything on that lovely clean screen of yours, you're probably going to have to do some reading.

To the library!

Once there, take out books with the determination of a contestant on *Supermarket Sweep*. You told your funders you were going to research 'representations of visual impairment in literature', because it sounded impressive, so grab anything you can find about eyes and the lack of eyes and representations of the lack of eyes and *How to do a PhD* and anything with a pretty cover.

Blimey, aren't books heavy? You'd never noticed before.

When you lug the books down to the front desk, hot and sweaty in your cardigan, ask the librarian: 'What's the maximum number of books I can take out in one go?' 'I don't know for a PhD,' he will say. 'But it's a lot.'

Smile and look at the queue behind you, hoping everyone heard that. *I don't know for a PhD*, he said. *For a PhD*. That's right, folks: a PhD! Ask for a plastic bag to put the books in and step outside into the rain.

At home, decide you are going to need a special shelf. Box up your self-help books and put your PhD books in their place. Sit at your desk and look at the shelf.

Make a cup of tea.

Watch *The Apprentice* on iPlayer.

Wonder what the term 'original research' means.

Go out to a nightclub with your friends and dance to the A-Team theme music.

Three days later, go to the special shelf, take a book, and begin to read. The book is about blind chimpanzees in Central Africa. Decide to write a PhD on 'The correlation between visually impaired chimpanzees in Central Africa and blind characters in the early novels of Charles Dickens'. Because it sounds impressive.

Open a new Word document and write that down. Then spend two and a half hours googling for correlations between visually impaired chimpanzees in Central Africa and blind characters in the early novels of Charles Dickens. Huh, well how about that? No luck.

*

Whew, you have just attended your sixth supervisor meeting, and thank goodness these exist.

Your supervisor has asked you to stop creating Word documents containing impressive-sounding titles, and to spend your time reading instead. 'Your angle will come,' he says mysteriously, and you can't help blushing at his use of the word come.

Decide that you are probably in love with your supervisor. Treat yourself to a new cardigan for your next meeting.

*

It is now half a year since you started, and your deliciously handsome supervisor has suggested you apply for a scholarship to study at the Library of Congress for a few months. In America. Five hundred and thirty eight miles of books, he says, and you picture the two of you, running naked through the English Literature section, kissing by Milton and boning by Chaucer.

Miraculously, your application for a scholarship is successful, and you fly out to Capitol Hill. There, you live with two guys; one of whom is a furniture salesman, and the other of whom works in Congress. It is the start of summer, and every time you step out of the door you feel like you are being slapped in the face with a hot, wet flannel. Throw away those cardigans, girlfriend!

At the library, there is a special Center ('er'), where you have your own workspace, and there is a filter coffee machine, and you have to get your bags checked every day on the way in and out, and you feel Very Important Indeed.

Go for beers after work with your new academic friends. Get so drunk you lose your way home and fall asleep on the steps of the Capitol building. Get found by the police. When they ask where you live, tell them you can't remember. (It starts with a … no, wait …) Let them take your phone and call your housemate, telling him to come and collect you. As he drives you back home at four in the morning, don't forget to tell him how sorry you are, at least once every five seconds. And cry as hard as you can when he informs you that you were asleep under his office window.

Spend the next day in bed, phoning your ex-boyfriend, your mother, your father, your sister, your friends. Get back with your ex-boyfriend, because a long-distance relationship is probably just what you need.

What you also need is routine: so find one. Arrive at the library for half nine. Leave at four. Read voraciously. Develop an interest in the representation of blind women in nineteenth-century literature. Come up with a groundbreaking theory about the description of prostitutes' eyes in the novels of Charles Dickens. Email your supervisor. Consider ending it with a kiss.

Spend evenings listening to your housemates debating politics. Understand about one sentence in ten. Go to a peacock farm owned by the furniture salesman's aunt. Lie on a sun-lounger by the pool and wonder whether getting back with your ex-boyfriend was a good idea.

*

Holy guacamole! You have a full draft of your PhD!

Near the end of the scholarship, your dad comes to visit you. Proudly show him your place at the library. Books here, computer there, filter coffee machine over there. Take him to the Brown Bag Lunch and listen to your friend Guido play a tune on the library's Stradivarius. Does your dad look impressed? Of course he does.

Take a couple of days out from the library to go to New Orleans with your dad. *Norlins*, he tells you. You have to pronounce it *Norlins*. Listen to a jazz band on the Mississippi. Take a horse and cart ride around the French quarter. Visit the voodoo museum. Go on a boat ride and spot eight alligators.

On your dad's last night in America, stay up late discussing your PhD. Sparkle as he tells you how proud he is. Listen carefully as he tells you how bored he gets these days, because he has no one to talk to about clever things. Ask him if that's why he drinks so much. Get him to promise to see a doctor about his hernia when he gets back. Tell him you love him more than anyone else in the world.

*

When you get back to Scotland, break up with your ex-boyfriend. Shortly after that get a phonecall from your dad. His hernia is sorted, he says, but now he has cancer.

*

See a psychiatrist.

Fly to Disneyworld with a man you have known for just two days. Then Prague with a man you have known two weeks. Consider this progress. Receive feedback from your supervisor. Edit. Edit.

See a psychologist.

*

Go to England and feel shocked at how ill your dad looks. Think about quitting your PhD. He tells you how proud he is of you for doing it, so don't quit, don't ever quit, just keep on going.

Back in Scotland, double your dose of antidepressants. Stop eating properly. Cry after two glasses of wine. Get herpes. Completely rewrite your entire PhD in a fortnight. (You have ditched the early nineteenth century, and are now looking exclusively at the fin de siècle. The fin de siècle is where it's at, dude.) Get a new boyfriend. Watch endless episodes of *Come Dine With Me* but stop cooking. Realise you're not really sure what the fin de siècle actually *is*. Return all your library books and put the self-help books back in their place.

How to Cope with Depression.
A Rough Guide to Grief.
Pulling Your Own Strings.

Phone home several times a day. Your mum tells you she wants a divorce. Your sister tells you she wants to die. Your dad tells you he has ten weeks to live.

Try cognitive behavioural therapy. Come off the antidepressants. Ask your supervisor out on a date and cry when he says no. Cry after one glass of wine. Tell your supervisor he is a total prick. (But delete the email before you hit send.) Rewrite the entire PhD again, this time only using words beginning with the letter 'c'. Come home early from a nightclub and cut yourself with a razor. Tear off a piece of the aloe vera plant and squeeze the gel onto your wound. Go back on the antidepressants. Develop a headache. Go for a brain scan.

Hurray for you, hurray for you.

Make a list of your losses over the last ten years. Map them out on A3 paper and colour-code them. Brain scan tests inconclusive. Go home for Father's Day. Decorate the patio in chalk. Draw hearts and stars and write 'I love you Graham's number' and tie balloons and streamers to the silver birch tree by the back door. Watch your dad walk across the patio with his zimmer frame and tears in his eyes.

Just before you leave, your dad whispers something: go on lots of adventures for me.

Cry on the train all the way back to Glasgow.

Move in with your boyfriend. Phone your dad and ask his advice on plastering walls. Wish him luck for his hospital appointment tomorrow.

Build a bed.

Find a missed call from your mum the next morning.

Seven hours later, arrive at the train station. Buy a cheese and onion sandwich for your dad and head for the hospital. Wonder why your mum has stopped replying to your texts. Walk through the hospital wondering where all the people are. Find the oncology ward and reach for the door handle. A nurse stops you. 'Haven't you heard?'

In a darkened room, you see your sister and your aunt and uncle. Your mum is waiting for you outside the wrong hospital entrance.

A few moments later, see your first dead body. Touch it. Talk to it. Say goodbye to it.

*

Drink. Cry. Edit.

*

It's snowing outside. Put on a cardigan. Fuck it, put on two.

Buy an extra pair of tights because your legs sting so badly in the cold, then walk tentatively towards your viva. A viva is an exam where you get to discuss the research you've done over the last four years. To show the examiners why you are an expert, why you deserve to be a Doctor. It's the most satisfying part of your whole PhD, your dad once told you.

Two hours later, the viva is over.

Try not to slip over in the snow on the way out, and head for the nearest bar. All your friends are waiting for you. They have cards and presents, balloons and streamers. Down two glasses of champagne and open your presents.

What's wrong with a PhD composed entirely with words beginning with the letter 'c', you ask. What's wrong with those cunting cocks – can't they cope with the concept?

Consider writing a letter to Margaret Atwood or Bill Gates. Consider writing a letter to your dad, telling him how relieved you are he's not here to see you fail.

Hurray for you.

Wonder what the hell a PhD is anyway. Then do all that you know how to do. Write.

Marianne Boruch

Beauty

– at the Hunterian Museum, London

Not clear or this quite. But here's a glass case
hunger made. How anything digests.
Tiny circuit boards
eked out of

>   lady bug
>
>   bumblebee
>
>   cricket   locust   leech.
>
>   One grasshopper. One.

Or a young crocodile, or that sea cucumber's
rubber band bits (no water, no wet, no blue,
no roaring). The intestinal worm's interior charms,
infinitesimal. A lizard
swallowed wildly too – a June bug took
that route, unlucky gnat after gnat after gnat.
The gastric runes of rat, of night heron, of reindeer.
The real inside skinny –
a single human fetus. On the spot
quiet. Middle shelf. For grandeur, for humility,
shock wired case-in-point.

Repeat sideways. To idle is to dream
by analogy. Something

like that. The one
could be many. Each dark night of little
gut machinery, same
turning thing into that other thing. Enter
leaf, root, flesh of world great and recognisable, mangled,
profoundly *stranged*, soaked, crushed
through gorgeous tubes, brilliant pockets to lift wings
minutes longer, a buzzing
made loud, claws gripping hard sand, hair to grow,
wounds to heal and vanish to
all right again. And rumblings so
raw, we who think we think this side of glass
beauty – no,

danger, go first.
I mean I love enough my own
false prophets of supper and air, lost daily
down that channel once

newt small, still trigger-sharp as a silkworm's
sprung, about to,
ravenous –
you hear yourself.

Knowledge

The glassy 8-ball floating up its cheap prophecy
yes   no   try later,
a white triangle, the black letters.
I did try. Spring, or it was
summer, me in my shorts on the sidewalk,
making my pact. There's time, this lasting forever.
Never childhood to a child.

We lose names of things. Then the things
they named. O Babylonians,
who slaughtered the sheep so its smoke turned prayer.
Praise, or a bribe.
What they really wanted--the liver,
organ of all-knowing,
in a temple, out of the sun.

One mark – you,
by yourself, always. Two marks: you earn
your enemy. Three: good news! he's
dust. Opposition is all. So is endurance.
That blue-gray lesion? The river will burn black.

More to read right in that flesh: desire,
motive, the usual damage to
greater damage. Don't – a very very dark in the left lobe.
Famine turns up
white as a rash, a speckling. The zones – for real –

Station and *Palace Gate* and *Path*.
Or my favorite, *Yoke and Increase*. You have to be
part optimist, like: fate equals bad,
destiny, not so bad.

In Anatomy, in lab, I did see a student
lift out a human liver.
Careful. Her gloved hands rose from the mess of his body.
Not love, that pause: to be
amazed by. They kept reading
a faint stain
to follow down. Fate behind the pillars
where something fell.
He probably thought future like we all think
in our blur of intentions – a grand place,
an okay place.

The Pope Under Glass

The pope under glass, the body
of the pope, red embroidered slippers of a pope,
a pope's plush red beanie, the eyes
of the pope closed a minute or two and he's back
in Bergamo, in seminary, still Angelo
the unnumbered, his buddies
happy drunk in the next room and then
they're singing.

Above him it's bad news forever. Such a huge
St. Jerome framed, afloat on his
deathbed, ravaged as the guy under the bridge
in my town, the one wrapped in three
sleeping bags – standard long straggly hair, gray,
ditto the beard – whose sweet moments
mean it hasn't rained, hasn't snowed, a day, two days.
So the plastic dries out.

In Rome, this churchiest
church imaginable, vast dazzling hive long ago
built of honey and spit. Only it's quiet
up where that very skinny St Jerome
keeps dying in swaddling clothes fit
for a baby, where he'd eye with alarm the lion
lower left corner
if he hadn't once loosed a thorn

from that paw, and if you add wings, it's
really Mark, St Mark

who wouldn't hurt a leopard, who – vaguely now,
some woodcut? – morphs back
to a man writing out his gospel
with a feather, miscast
in luscious medieval robes. One skull.
And black ink on the table.
Or that was Jerome. Eternity's
not too accurate.

The pilgrims line up with earphones
that leak: muffled e-bits of Italian, smudge
of English, distant pinball of French
and Japanese. They file past
the glass coffin, arrange their faces reverently
to say nothing much, same exact
disappear in it. Pope John is

so white. There are chairs
if you want. I want, I want.
Next to me, a nun at her rosary,
her holy rumble
slow, not yet past a third Glory-be.
We've been here –
how many lifetimes does it take?
Five trillion. A guess.

Reviews

Memorial: An Excavation of the Iliad
Alice Oswald. Faber. ISBN 9780571274161. HBK. £12.99

'My desire in writing this piece is to achieve in musical terms the same sort of feeling one gets upon entering one of those old, majestic cathedrals in France or Italy [...] You feel you are in the presence of many souls, generations upon generations of them, and you sense their collected energy.' This is John Adams' account of his 2002 work for choir and orchestra *On The Transmigration of Souls* which commemorates the victims of the 9/11 atrocity. Adams' work opens unsettlingly on street sounds over which speaking voices read one by one the names of the dead – to become a polyphony of voices – the streaming litany of names interspersed with texts taken from missing-persons signs. Throughout this 'memory space' the composer felt 'no desire to create a musical "narrative" or description.' The similarities with Alice Oswald's own memory space, hers a setting of Homer's *Iliad*, are obvious, not least in the poet's description of her approach to Homer's 'vocative poem' as 'a translation of the *Iliad*'s atmosphere, not its story [...] aiming for translucence rather than translation'. In this way, Oswald brings to light the *enargeia* of the *Iliad*, its 'bright unbearable reality'.

It follows that the experience of Oswald's poem is a profoundly musical one; just as Adams transports us across artistic barriers, pushing out the boundaries of 'music' to include noise', Oswald's translation stunningly reveals the music of words and, moreover, the modulating, dynamic music of their meanings. In the same way that Oswald's *Dart* (2002) was a 'map poem or song line', *Memorial* is composed for the listening ear, the sound of thinking audible throughout: 'like the changing mind / That moves a cloud off a mountain' as one of her similes seizes it. It seems to me deeply important then that *Memorial* is available not only in published book form but as a CD audio book read by the author. To hear Oswald's performance is a gripping musical event, particularly in the way that the sounds of the Greek names, left untranslated, are faithfully enunciated; cities such as 'Pyrasus Iton Pteleus Antron', Tarne and, of course, endlessly throughout, those of the dead. As in Adams' memory space, the names are voiced one by one at the poem's beginning, a line dedicated to each one, as the space around, the silence of the page, rings out: *Me-ne-lay'-us* (Menelaus), *Me-reye'-o-neez* (Meriones), *E-le-fee'nor* (Elephenor). The macaronic music of the Greek language carries the reading ear along, the energetic frisson between words revivifying English expression and our own thinking with it.

As one listens and lives again and again through Oswald's *Memorial*, one remembers Anne Carson's 2010 elegy for her brother, *Nox*, in which she, much like Oswald, attempts to 'gather up the shards of his story and make it into something containable.' Carson is also a trained classicist and *Nox* is a carrying over into English of Catullus' Roman elegy CI. Somehow, as Carson understands, the probing act of translation seems to go to the heart of the dark, heavy spaces of grieving where words must be searched out and turned over: 'I came to think of translating as a room, not exactly an unknown room, where one gropes for the light switch. I guess it never ends. [...] Prowling the meanings of a word, prowling the history of a person, no use expecting a flood of light.' Oswald's own description of *Memorial* as an 'excavation' of the *Iliad* restores to us the roots of that word in Latin: 'from excavare to hollow out [...] see cave' and its dictionary definition: 'To make hollow by removing the inside [...] to dig out (soil) leaving a hollow [...] to form into by hollowing.' The process of grieving, which never ends, is a slow, studied one of sifting and digging, of looking deeply and questioningly into the meanings of the words and the thought-patterns by which we live. Indeed, one of the most harrowing statements in Adams' *Transmigration*, that of the sister of one of the 9/11 dead, fuses grieving with digging: 'I wanted to dig him out. I know just where he is.' At one early point in *Nox*, as she interrogates the etymology of the word 'history' (from ancient Greek meaning 'to ask') Carson reminds us of how 'history and elegy are akin': 'It is when you are asking about something that you realise you yourself have survived it, and so you must carry it, or fashion it into a thing that carries itself.'

The form of *Memorial* is a hollowing out, the poem an echo-chamber construction, and it is the noise that strikes one first, breaking upon the ears as the impetus of repetition creates a profoundly propulsive energy, an alliterative charge:

> The first to die was Protesilaus
> A focused man who hurried to darkness
> With forty black ships leaving the land behind
> Men sailed with him from those flower-lit cliffs
> Where the grass gives growth to everything

Throughout, Oswald develops Homer's use of epic simile across the expanse of the work as all of her expertly-turned similes are delivered twice. One effect of this double sounding is to force the reader into closely attending to single words, to become conscious of how they, as we, move in time. 'To exist in time is necessarily to exist in repetition', James Longenbach has identified. According to Oswald, her repeated similes provide a 'break from the grief', even a 'sense of healing.' But this seems too consolatory. Rather, it seems to me, repetition intensifies the loss, emptying words of meaning and easy identification. There is a profound and uncrossable disconnect between the tenor and the vehicle – after all, to be 'like' is not to be precisely the same thing – a gap that we are moved to find our way through as we are lifted out into the unknowns of language and reality. To quote Longenbach once again: 'Language becomes a place where we live [...] hovering between the literal and the figurative.' These are the slippages, the unfillable silences of translation. Words repeated become mere sound, amplifying absence, the absence of meaning and of human life – as in Walt Whitman's elegy for Lincoln and its repetition of the word 'Death, death, death, death, death'. Pulled into experiencing repetition we are pulled into the workings of memory, each simile becoming intimately part of our own experience of reality through language.

Oswald's investment in epic similes illuminates the oral nature of the poem, bringing the Homeric voice across the centuries' distances to us. Thus, in the *Iliad* we get Agamemnon in Book IX 'streaming tears like a dark spring running down / some desolate rock face, its shaded currents flowing' and this is repeated later in the work as Patroclus in Book XV weeps 'warm tears like a dark spring running down'. Repetition serves to make audible the conscious voice of the thinking, remembering poet shaping and working the material and, by extension, the presence of the voice in, the vocative element of, the poem. Words are spoken and in this way they live. Moreover, the repetition of words and motifs impresses upon us the repetitive force of death, of war as death falling upon death as snow falls, night must fall and leaves fall. An inexorable process takes over as we are made to feel the relentless motion of words over the poetic lines, of words in time: 'Like leaves who could write a history of leaves / The wind blows their ghost to the ground / And the spring breathes new leaf into the woods'. This, one of the stand-alone similes that closes Oswald's work, brings history and Homer to us, as it echoes closely the words spoken in Book VI of the *Iliad* by Glaucus to Diomedes in the no man's land between armies: 'Like the generation of leaves, the lives of mortal men [...] as one generation comes to life, another dies away'.

For Carson translation is 'not a recovery of the past' but 'another layer of us playing with the past' in which the poet must, crucially, 'leave the spaces'.

Atmospherics then and not story – indeed Oswald's extended improvisation is much truer to the idea of 'war music' than Christopher Logue's work of that title also based on the *Iliad*. Elsewhere, in her essay 'Variations on the Right to Remain Silent', Carson reminds us of how, in the practice of translation, 'Silence is as important as words'. Alive to the heft of words, their music, the surrounding silences, this valedictory 'valleyful of voices' is a triumph of the composing, creative imagination in which the poet has each word sound its own particular grief or weight (the verb 'grieve' comes from *gravis,* heavy). Across this 'excavation' the poetic simile shines in perpetuity, each one opening up onto the vast, dizzying spaces of language, as the names of the dead, all passing facts of long ago, all mortal, become eternally part of the colossal, empty universe in which we too find ourselves for a time. As Wordsworth apprehended in his elegy for Lucy, all 'rolled round in earth's diurnal course / with rocks and stones and trees'.

Maria Johnston

Charles Dickens: A Life. Viking. ISBN 9780670917679. HBK £30
Claire Tomalin

Claire Tomalin's life of Dickens is a substantial, well-argued and well-arranged survey of the author which might bring back to Dickens many of those who had perhaps dismissed him as a Victorian phenomenon of lesser interest today. Not so: the book's skilful deployment of material (backed by compact and very well presented evidence), its use of the magisterial Pilgrim edition of the letters, and above all its continuous thread of good narration makes a hefty (well over 500 pages) story well worth reading, and reintroduces the reader to an author whose sheer energy and output make it hard to see how even 500 pages could do him justice. Like Jenny Hartley's recent *Selected Letters* (Oxford), Claire Tomalin's *Life* operates through selection, arrangement and minimal authorial intrusion. Not that Tomalin is absent: her longstanding interest in Dickens's women (*The Invisible Woman: The Story of Nelly Ternan and Charles Dickens*) means that the *Life* does justice to the troubled later years of the Dickens marriage, and above all the extraordinary extent to which Dickens contrived to keep the secret of his affair secret for so long, and after it became public property to conduct a second, parallel life to his public one under a false name ('Charles Tringham'); stolen weekends and short holidays with Nelly meticulously tracked here, with due acknowledgement of how well he covered his tracks, and how much has to be supposition. Those present at his death may have included Nelly: Tomalin has used the most recent researches, as well as her own library work and interviews, but she never pushes the material further than suggestion. The Dickens of these pages is fraught with ill-suppressed energy, his love for his wife obvious in letters, his impatience and his sexual frustrations equally so. Here is a man driven by early acquaintance with poverty to rise socially through the almost impenetrable ranks of Victorian England; a man always short of money as more and more family members attached themselves to his exchequer; a juggler who could keep serial novels on the workbench while editing magazines, organising theatricals, giving speeches, and above all public readings in the UK and in North America, while pouring forth the correspondence which we know was greater than the twelve Pilgrim volumes since a good deal has been destroyed. The man was obviously driven.

How to organise the material from letters, research, interview, reviews, the work of Victorian contemporaries? This is where Tomalin has laid the foundation of her success. Beginning with a cast of characters from her account, and maps to illustrate the localities, she divides Dickens's story into three distinct and very successful sections which help the reader hold on to the wealth of detail as Dickens whizzes through his career. The early years – the appalling financial mismanagement of his father, the blacking factory, the prentice years of reporting and writing – are lightly done. Then in part two, 'As he approached his twenty-eighth birthday in February, Dickens knew himself to be famous, successful and tired.' This biography (it has a nice turn of phrase throughout) pins its subject with that remark: the desire to be famous and successful is the driver from an early age, the human cost to himself (and those around him) immense, only the frenetic energy and restlessness keeping him going. Trying out reading aloud the scene where Bill Sykes murders Nancy on Catherine his wife, she 'was reduced to "an unspeakable '*state*'", he informed Forster with great satisfaction'. The germ of many a successful future public reading, perhaps, which reduced both reader and audience to a *state*. And note the appearance early in the work of John Forster, Dickens's confidant and friend, business and commercial associate, critic and guide – throughout his career Dickens was to rely on Forster's company and companionship, and the letters occasionally show how important he found it to have someone he could confess his moments of loneliness and uncertainty to. Not Catherine, certainly: the letters to her are full of affection, but for the real moments of confession and apologia, we turn to Forster. Strange that he should be pilloried as Podsnap in *Our Mutual Friend*, but Dickens's imagination was too wild to avoid a good chance for a comic character.

Part three ('Stormy Weather') begins in 1857 with the meeting with the Ternan family and its enormous consequences: 'the wing of a butterfly flapped, and a whole weather system was unsettled'. From that point, the biography skilfully conducts a double narrative, Dickens the creative genius, flogging his imagination and his body through exhaustion and illness to produce, produce – and Dickens the human being, spending more and more time with Nelly while treating Catherine really very badly. Somehow, in this period he manages to produce *Our Mutual Friend*, his last completed novel and his greatest. 'The scope of Dickens's observations is prodigious, and his satirical bite as sharp as a fresh razor,' says Tomalin, and she is right. It is hard to imagine how Dickens kept the serial parts of his novels in his mind as his life whirled in confusion, but he did, and he plunged into *Edwin Drood* with apparently undimmed energy. But in a bizarrely unfocused episode, he was to collapse and die midway, with conflicting accounts of where, when and in whose presence. As Victorian Britain prepared to bury one of its greatest geniuses in Westminster Abbey, the family tried to keep private the messiness of his private encounters. Dickens spoke even late in life of his 'usual gymnastic condition', but the strain of the gymnastics was formidable as he kept his public and private lives in precarious balance.

Tomalin comments briefly and pungently on the novels as she passes, and details slip out which illuminate – Dickens's mother wearing showy sables (Mrs Boffin?), Dickens's ability to create wonderful scenes from imagination even when the originals he sought (the Yorkshire schools he failed to inspect in *Nicholas Nickleby*, the cotton towns near Preston in *Hard Times*, cold and strike-bound when he saw them) failed him.

Tomalin's success here brings to mind *American Notes*, a superb example of sharp observation piled on observation, the whole thing threaded on a narrative. Her comments on her subject have bite: 'He wanted to be married. He did not want a wife who would compel his imagination.' … '*Great Expectations* … did not come from research or the theatre but out of a deep place in Dickens's imagination which he never chose to explain. And perhaps never could, and it is all the better for that. And perhaps Dickens himself on himself: "'*Restlessness*, you will say. Whatever it is, it is always driving me, and I cannot help it.'"

The picture achieves good balance. Dickens's failings as father and husband (himself the child of parents who were at best failures) are given full cover. Tomalin's research, corralled at the end of the book, is well controlled and deployed. The material on Nelly Ternan (evidence still coming to light) will come as a surprise to many. *Charles Dickens: A Life* is a handsome book, handsomely illustrated. The widespread praise it has earned is very well deserved.

Ian Campbell

Trackman. Luath Press. ISBN 1908373075 £9.99
Catriona Child

Trackman is an intriguing and slightly strange debut novel all about the therapeutic power of music, from an author who shows plenty of promise for the future, writing with a whole lot of heart, a good deal of empathy and no small amount of skill.

Like a lot of debut works, however, the passion of the author for his or her subject matter and characters tends to result in passages of overwriting, and on this evidence there is still plenty for Child to learn about self-editing and plot.

The novel is set in contemporary Edinburgh (well, more or less, we'll come to that in a bit), and the story is told through the eyes of Davie Watts, a young man drifting through life after the tragic and traumatic death of his younger brother Lewis. I won't go into the details of Lewis's death here, as the reader is ably drip-fed those details as the novel progresses, but suffice to say Davie feels responsible, rightly or wrongly, and he is clearly undergoing a period of some kind of post-traumatic stress disorder to compound his grief.

To add to his problems, he has dropped out of university and is working at a menial job in the Virgin Megastore on Princes Street (which is, of course, no longer there – a strange anachronism for a novel purporting to be set in the present day). Plus his parents have split up in the aftermath of Lewis's death, his mother moving to Australia and his father posted missing from Davie's life.

So our poor wee Davie doesn't have much going for him. He shares a flat with an egotistical musician called Alfie, he has had the odd dalliance with Martha, the emo from work, and he has a crush on Astrid, a gorgeous American student who is a regular customer in the store.

His only support network is Susan, his older cousin and a single mum, who doesn't have her own troubles to seek, an abusive ex-husband lurking in the wings to potentially cause problems throughout the book.

So Davie's life is ripe for an intervention, and he gets one, in the unlikely shape of a magic MP3 player handed to him by a homeless guy he knows only as The One Dread Guy. The MP3 player initially seems broken, but Davie is strangely compelled to keep it, and as he drifts around Edinburgh, the player tells him to get random strangers to listen to it, and somehow magically provides the perfect song for these distressed punters to hear at that particular moment to sort their lives out.

And so Davie helps a wide cross-section of Edinburgh turn their lives around, from the young girl dumped by her boyfriend to an elderly man suffering from cancer, from a pubescent Travis fan questioning his sexuality to a kids party and the assorted troubled parents present.

It's a neat idea, and Child handles it well, but I'm not altogether convinced it's an idea that has legs for an entire novel, certainly not one of 350 pages. After the initial set-up, *Trackman* does begin to feel a little too episodic, and there's nothing much driving the narrative forwards until much nearer the end, as Davie gets further and further into a personal hole, yet becomes obsessed with helping others, leading to an inevitable epiphany on the Forth Road Bridge.

The one thing that *Trackman* does have in spades is charm, and that can carry a narrative a long way. Davie's voice is not always likeable but it always seem true to his character, which is always the most important thing, and his interactions with those around him, especially with the love interests Martha and Astrid, are well handled and solidly believable.

Interestingly for a female author, the women characters in *Trackman* are a lot thinner than the men. Martha and Astrid are exactly that – love interests and little more, serving only as facilitators for Davie's state of mind changes. And his cousin Susan isn't much deeper, something of a standard single mum stereotype.

Another minor quibble on my part would be the songs that Child has chosen as her epiphany tunes for Davie's random strangers. There is something very safe and middle of the road about them, making it hard to believe they would be life-changing moments, and it's difficult to find a song recorded in the last five years (the kids' party excepted) which, along with that anachronistic Virgin Megastore, makes the book feel somehow slightly out of date already.

But overall, *Trackman* is a good solid read and a well-executed piece of writing. What could've been schmaltzy or twee in other hands has been given more emotional undertow by Davie's tragic background, and I look forward to seeing what Child writes in the future.

Doug Johnstone

Note on Lighting a Fire. Happenstance Press. ISBN 9781905939718. HBK. £10
Gerry Cambridge

I went on a course at Cove Park the other week called 'Freeing The Poet's
Voice'. Voice-coach Kristin Linklater's aim was to make us, as self-conscious
(at best) performers of our own work, better acquainted with our vocal
apparatus, which turns out to consist (potentially) of the entire body. The
intensive four-day course of physical and emotional limbering up left me
with many memorable linguistic images ('voice is made of breath and bone')
but the insight that seemed to arrest all of us was Kristin's advice to 'get out
of the way of the poem'. I liked that. For the last few years I've been asking
myself about the difference between intention and inspiration (although
when people use the word 'inspiration' to me it usually makes me wince) in
the poetic impulse.

I will need not to get diverted into talking about our discoveries, which
I suspect will inform my writing, speaking and teaching for some time, but
I justify opening my review of *Notes on Lighting A Fire* with this preamble
because Gerry Cambridge attended Kristin's course in 2011, and I was
curious to see if I could see any influence of it in this collection.

Interviewed in *New Linear Perspectives*, Cambridge identifies his 'themes'
very tidily as:

> fascination with light, male experience in regard to aligning itself to what
> is female, my sense of astonishment in the face of the physical reality
> of the universe we live in, and at the transformations which have to take
> place within it [...] A new thing, though, is the concern with family.

Business-like! I get that readers do like to know what a book is about before
they read it, and that a poetry collection's 'themes' can look deceptively very
clear in retrospect of writing, but I've wondered if in this case their clarity is
symptomatic of a distracting self-consciousness throughout the book.

At its opening, Cambridge instructs his reader or himself in the laying of
a fire. Even allowing the conceit to be a conceit, the tone is teacherly: 'The
biggest coals to the bottom, mind[...] Place these fastidiously about on the
kindling/like punctuation'. The poem closes with permission to enjoy the
results, and 'settle/to the scratch of a pen in praise of primordial fire'. I can't
imagine much less primordial than this particular concretion of language, for
all it exhibits the poet's typical elegance and transparency.

Cambridge is otherwise articulate about what I think I'll need to call *life-force* in this book which is flushed with sap, yolk and blood – 'the bloody pulsing brain beneath' ('Exposure'). Some of the poetry is so viscerally acute that often, on first reading, my reaction was a gag-reflex, as in 'At Twelve' when he describes blowing out 'the eggs/of blackies and thrushes and linnets/cored with blood and jelly', and with that characteristic sense of guilt:

> if the egg was fresh as it should be,
> the pumping gold of what would now
> be no singing bird.

His 'alignment' of 'the hot uprush of spring and sex', of 'the helpless look of a hen blackbird, glazed wide eye and beak and tail' with 'the girls as if they had given/a wisp of a secret away' made me cringe but, especially in the wake of 'Freeing The Poet's Voice', I'm inclined to interpret these reactions as telling muscular ones, signifying that even if I don't relish the perspective, they are at least honest. This sequence is powerful stuff, when Cambridge doesn't 'get in its way'. When he does, the poems are justified with a moral whose purpose seems to be to absolve the guilt of the child – 'It's the look I remember most today' ('At Twelve'). Unencumbered in this way, you get such aurally-exquisite veracity as:

> the big fierce rust-blotched egg in a sweating palm
> on a doomy evening in the windy woods with a storm
> crackling [...]
> oh it was primitive! A sparrowhawk's egg,
> a bartered death that said *I live! I live!*

I get a kick out of the poet striding about like a Jarl 'Blood-faced, stamping through/that creaking dazzle and that rare blue' ('Young Snow'), his near-fetishised newly-shaven head 'a hot thin soil for rain' ('Exposure'), embracing colour and weather and in this mood I experience some of the body-in-voice that both Cambridge and I have explored with Kristin Linklater, although I doubt the poems are a consequence of the course. His percussive and onomatopoeic vocabulary has the tone of Viking kennings and is forged from various ores including Ayrshire Scots – 'wince-light of the blintering days' and 'egreted marshes/gloating in the glaur and spawn' and 'Duskalldaylight' ('Little Light Psalm').

I'm not saying that I need a poet to have one subject-matter and one voice to articulate it in, but in this mode, Cambridge is less likely to anthropomorphise flamingoes as 'bibulous retired colonels/with boxers' broken noses/who happen to be cross-dressers'. Or to deaden the music of the poetry with stolid adverbs, as in 'Awakening' – 'satisfyingly meaty'; 'fascinatedly crowding', 'progressiving mysteriously'.

In the *New Linear Perspectives* interview, he expresses the belief that 'you also have to allow the reader to meet you at times, imaginatively, halfway.' I would take that further and say, if you don't let your reader make their own way into every poem, they may not be willing to wade in at all. If you order me to 'Look –' or 'Listen!' to the 'miles-wide disco of amphibian music' I may well choose to shut my eyes and stop my ears, which might or might not be more than my own thrawnness.

Cambridge does mention a further 'ambition' in that interview – 'for [the poems] to have in addition that indefinable quality [...] George Mackay Brown would have called "a thread too bright for the eye".' Despite my complaints about Cambridge blocking the signal, if you like, this thread does blaze finely through many of these poems. I'm glad to own the book for the peculiar and delicate 'Processional at the Winter Solstice', and the best of the birdnesting poems such as 'Blowing Out an Egg' and 'A Sparrowhawk's Nest'. And 'The Queen' – in which the obsession with light and Deep Time is fulfilled without being abstracted:

> In the flex and pulse of her abdomen are stored
> Ten thousand summer wasps, wasp dynasties
> Down the perpetual light of centuries;
> And she will be adored.

In this poem, Cambridge keeps his word ('I only want to briefly look at her') by stepping back from the 'clear cell on my kitchen sill' and letting nature take over:

> It is Easter Sunday; she wants to begin
> Her own fierce story of resurrection
> Though they would kill her still,
> Those bleak gusts of March,
> And that high, wasp-heedless blue.

Jen Hadfield

Stranger Magic. Charmed States & the Arabian Nights. Chatto & Windus.
ISBN 9780701173319. HBK. £28
Marina Warner

In the fourteenth-century Syrian manuscript containing one gathering
of the story cycles which grew into what Western literary culture would
eventually call the *Arabian Nights*, storytellers portray the wonder in which
their listeners will be entangled by recourse to a particular metaphor: the
tale, say several, should 'be engraved with needles at the corner of the eye',
a 'lesson' whose intricately strange beauty at the sheer narrative level is only
mirrored by the miraculous power of an expert calligrapher to inscribe it
on a tiny ocular canvas. However evisceratingly eye-watering the metaphor,
it sums up the *Nights'* glorious metafictionality. In the story of the second
dervish told on the fiftieth night, a king's daughter (who is about to do
shape-shifting battle with a demon) bespells by means of inscribing on a
floor magical words and patterns in ancient Arabic; just so the *Nights* itself
has been a talisman in Western culture inspiring, perplexing, and beguiling
artists, writers, poets, and filmmakers to create wonders of their own. In her
brilliant new book, Warner traces the drama of its enduring enchantment, a
process of reception, transformation, imitation, and recreation which enlists
the fictions of Scott and Stevenson, Irving and Poe, Diderot and Voltaire,
Borges and Calvino (for starters). This 'polyvocal echo chamber', to use
Warner's phrase, has been richly charted in the work of Robert Irwin and
others but *Stranger Magic* is singularly Warneresque in its excavation of the
artistic, social, political, scientific, and religious histories in which Western
European understanding of the *Nights* has been layered. As ever for Warner,
the question of the needful persistence of myth (in all its varieties) in this
supposedly disenchanted world returns; this time, the *Nights* provides her
with a way of thinking about what Borges calls 'reasoned imagination'. In the
Enlightenment and post-Enlightenment eras, the *Nights* may have safely but
troublingly bedecked magic in Orientalist guise but, Warner argues, the work
also embodies and enacts forms of 'magical thinking' which are expressive of
'processes inherent to human consciousness and connected to constructive
and imaginative thought'.

From its very inception, the *Nights* resisted categorisation or containment.
'Polymorphous' and 'arabesque', adjectives by which Warner describes its
story cycles, aptly sums up the history of its transformations through print,
culture, and language. Once upon a time these stories belonged to Indian,

Persian, and Arabic oral cultures from at least the ninth and tenth centuries before emerging into two divergent manuscript sources in Syrian and Egyptian tradition. Somehow this process of transmigration from oral into print mediums – which in other contexts can mean the death of a tradition or indigenous culture – is inventively self-renewing. At the start of the eighteenth century, Antoine Galland tried to pin a kind of fixity on the great story-sprawl by translating and publishing it in French but not before adding two of the tales for which the *Nights* is particularly now celebrated: *Aladdin* and *Ali-baba*. It is a lovely irony in the twisted threads of the *Nights'* history that the iconic genie and the lamp should come from a Syrian storyteller, Hanna Diyab, whom Galland had heard perform the tales; he knew that these fictions – fairy tales *à la orientale* – would transform a contemporary literary culture with a rapacious love for extravagant fictions. The *Nights* is not only a begetter of imaginative and cultural renewal but, as Warner reminds us at the start, woven through its very fabric are affirmations of the life-renewing, or life-prolonging, power of stories. The frame storyteller, Shahrazad, insists on becoming a narrator in order to frustrate a king's murderous intent. Distracted from the horror of his misogynistic revenge plan (since he believes all women unfaithful and corrupt, he will successively marry, then kill, a bride each day), he discovers an insatiable desire for stories (a Bluebeard redeemed by the salvific power of female creativity). These are tales which are broken, interrupted, fragmented across nights, leaving plots, narratives, and conversations adrift (such as that between the she-ghoul and the king's son on the fifteenth night) as Shahrazad falls silent at daybreak; when she beckons 'Listen' as darkness gathers, her gesture inaugurates a scene of storytelling re-enacted throughout medieval and Renaissance frame narratives, and a nocturnality which imbued the *Nights* with an illicit and phantasmagoric eroticism.

As a virtuosically 'broken' narrative, it has a cultural after-life which is itself in bedazzling pieces but it is Warner's gift that she constructs them together in overarching and illuminating ways (her narrative, too, is polyphonic but its five key conceptual sections make an arc). One of its centrifugal points is the *Nights'* relationship to Orientalism, since it has been subject to a series of Occidental misreadings and misappropriations (such as post-Napoleonic Egyptomania, British Gothic fantasy, Decadent and Symbolist utopias, and filmic representation from *The Thief of Baghdad* to Disney's *Aladdin*) which fossilise, essentialise, and exoticise. For a start, as Warner illustrates, the alluring 'stranger magic' of the *Nights* – the 'coarsened' fantasy of Oriental otherness which was spun in the largely Judaeo-Christian context of reception

– belies the intricacy, depths, and gradations of magical practice and belief in Eastern philosophy and science exemplified by the magicians, demons, and jinn of the stories. Warner suggests a different reconfiguration of influence and inspiration: 'the scholars and artists who observed and documented – and sectioned and measured – the things of the East encountered something which they recognised as a sign of their own changing relationship to things, and that what they learned can be instructive in our times as well'. This is the prelude to one of the richest chapters in the book which explores the 'various enchanted paraphernalia' of the *Nights* – the extraordinary detailed and 'living' materiality of objects and artefacts. Her discussion of the instrumentality of magic and the consciousness of things/objects in the *Nights* – those 'ambiguous phenomena' which made Coleridge as a child feel relieved when daylight fell on his copy of the *Nights* – freshly illuminates in particular the animism of Andersen's fairy tales.

If this forms one neglected dimension of the West's cognitive and emotional responses to the *Nights,* then the space of magical thinking in modernity offers another vivid example of 'emancipatory imagination'. In the book's final section, Warner brilliantly analyses the ways in which the *Nights* – always bound up with spectacle (not least, and almost simultaneously, in the arts of the Ballets Russes, pantomime, music hall, and circus extravaganza), and with modes of psychological non-conformism – fires the 'cinematic dreaming' of the twentieth century. There is a beautiful exposition of the silent fairytale films of the Berlin filmmaker, Lotte Reiniger. Like a modern Shahrazad, she fashioned a *Tricktisch* (a contraption which was her own specially devised animation studio) to bring shadow puppets alive in a skein of dream experiences and states of consciousness – a skein which, as Warner's book tells us, runs by virtue of the *Nights*' uncanny (mis)understandings from Enlightenment culture to psychoanalysis (not for nothing, it seems, did Freud drape *Die Couch* in an oriental rug; the *Nights*' flying carpet was prescient) to contemporary technological phantasmagoria.

Fairy tales need not be utopian but the *Nights* has an optimism, and so too does Warner's book. A chapter is devoted to Goethe's *West-Östlicher Divan* [The West-Eastern Divan], an imitation of and paean to Persian and Arabic poetic lyricism; an Orientalist masquerade but one borne out of a context of political struggle and resistance and, for this reason perhaps, why Edward Said and Daniel Barenboim named their Arab–Israeli youth orchestra after it. Warner is both in disagreement and sympathy with Said throughout *Stranger Magic* because for her the shifting fabulisms within, and inspired by, the *Nights* culturally and linguistically reconfigure the preoccupations of modernity 'towards an ethical vision'. 'The research for this book began during the first Gulf War, and continued during the many, appalling and unresolved conflicts in the regions where the *Nights* originated', she tells us at the end; 'I wanted to present another side of the culture cast as the enemy and an alternative history to vengeance and war.' In suggesting other ways to look at the *Nights'* vast cultural seedings in the West, this is a scholarship with humanity, and as sharp as the art of that ocular calligrapher.

Sarah Dunnigan

The Age of Miracles. Simon & Schuster. ISBN 9780857207234. HBK. £14.99
Karen Thompson Walker

Karen Thompson Walker's seductive first novel is an ordinary story about the trials and tribulations of a Californian sixth grader, Julia, told by her adult self. Like many good coming of age novels, there's nostalgia and uncertainty on every page. But Julia's reminiscences are sadder and more potent, because her story takes place in the first year of 'the slowing' – a colossal event that makes the earth's days longer and seems to have set the planet on course for extinction.

Released somewhat ominously on the longest day of the year, Thompson Walker's debut has been tipped as 2012's publishing sensation since being sold to Simon & Schuster for half a million pounds in a highly competitive auction. Some commentators have already made connections between the book and the earthquake and tsunami of March 2011, which reportedly shifted the earth's tilt slightly and made our days a couple of millionths of a second shorter.

But unlike that event, whose memory is dominated by images of nuclear doom and boats stranded miles inland, Thompson Walker's disaster is largely, as Julia puts it, 'a quite invisible catastrophe'. For a mysterious, unexplained reason, the earth's rotation begins to slow. Days begin to get longer, initially by minutes, then by hours, until eventually the sun does not set for many weeks. At first, it's a hard premise to swallow: our concept of time is so fixed and rigid that the idea of one day lasting more than twenty-four hours seems too far-fetched, even a little ridiculous. But Julia's tale quickly forms a compelling narrative that highlights how important ordinary childhood experiences are in extraordinary times.

In slow, sometimes painstaking detail, Julia reflects upon her sixth grade life: her clumsiness with her changing body; her parents' fights; her yearning for quiet, handsome skateboarder Seth; her heartbreak when her best friend moves away. But it's a memoir punctuated by details of the slowing: the weirdness of sticking to a twenty-four-hour clock during a forty-eight-hour day, the threat of food shortages, the tensions that arise between those that keep 'clock time' and 'real time' which threaten to erupt into violence.

Thompson Walker's writing is magnetic and drips with foreboding on every page. Her novel straddles the genres of science fiction and young adult literature, emulating the dystopian anxiety of books with as wide appeal as Ray Bradbury's *Fahrenheit 451* and Suzanne Collins' *The Hunger Games*. But it's cinematic too, like a low-budget disaster movie. The first chapter reads almost like a film trailer, ending with a potential tagline: 'there was nowhere on earth to go'. So it's not hard to see why publishers fought so hard to secure *The Age of Miracles*: it's accessible and easily digestible but smart, and gives new meaning to the offhand desire for more hours in a day.

Essentially, it's this down-to-earth quality that makes *The Age of Miracles* such an impressive book. Thompson Walker, a former editor for Simon & Schuster in New York, is a lean writer – like Cormac McCarthy but with pathos and commas. Her prose smacks of someone who has read and edited many books, who knows what hooks readers in and what turns them away.

That's not to say *The Age of Miracles* is immaculately written. Its captivating rhythm is occasionally knocked off kilter by unnecessary hyperbole – like 'How could we have known that the workings of the universe had finally made appropriate the fire of my mother's words?' – and the odd misjudged simile: 'My mother [was] convinced that danger, like potatoes, breeds in the dark.'

Moreover, there's a noticeable lack of humour in the novel. No one really tells jokes, or lightens the apocalyptic atmosphere. This distinct absence of laughter – even in the face of impending doom – doesn't ring true. Likewise, the slowing is given too much credit for events that unfold in Julia's life, even the most ordinary of human emotions. Birds falling out of the sky may be a believable consequence of the earth's slowing rotation. But a rash decision made by Julia's usually level-headed father could perhaps be more credibly blamed on panic in the face of adversity, rather than the 'subtler psychological shifts that also accompanied the slowing'.

There's also a frustrating lack of scientific explanation for the slowing and its aftermath which, when the allure of reading the novel is over, weakens its memory and distances it from our reality. Still, it's a first-rate debut that simultaneously feels refreshing yet comfortingly familiar. Thompson Walker plays the hope of childhood against the hopelessness of the earth's predicament and in leaving us with the personal tragedies of her fictional apocalypse – families shattered, relationships left unfulfilled, childhood sweethearts bereft of a happy ending – invites us to appreciate our days and nights while we can.

Yasmin Sulaiman

A Choosing: Selected Poems. Polygon. ISBN 9781846972225. PBK. £9.99
Liz Lochhead

At the launch of *A Choosing* at the 2011 Edinburgh International Book Festival, Liz Lochhead was keen to stress the importance of its name. 'It's a choosing,' she pointed out, noting that the title was not quite that of the much-loved poem from her debut collection, *Memo for Spring*. 'It's not *the* choosing. I think that's quite important.' Why? Because, she claimed, she wanted her selection to be instinctive, natural. 'Another day, another year, I might have made quite a different selection,' she says in the Author's Note. 'I don't want to say too much about the poems in this book except: here they are.' The message is typical of Lochhead's philosophy: poetry should not be picked over or scrutinised too much. It should simply be enjoyed.

The reader's enjoyment certainly seems to be the focus of this *Selected*. As perhaps any volume of selected poems should aim to do, the book functions as a greatest hits album, featuring many of Lochhead's best-known works. The reader is reintroduced to familiar characters: the small child frightened by the bull in 'Revelation'; the overbearing mother-in-law of the many-times-anthologised 'My Rival's House'; and of course, 'Everybody's Mother' with its brilliant punch-line, 'Nobody's mother can't not never do nothing right.' The poems are taken largely from Lochhead's most popular collections – the majority were originally published in *Memo for Spring* (1972), *The Grimm Sisters* (1981) and *Dreaming Frankenstein* (1984). Somewhat disappointingly, there are only four from the less-known *Bagpipe Muzak* (1991), and none at all from *True Confessions and New Clichés*, Lochhead's collection of raps and performance pieces published in 1985. (In the Author's Note, Lochhead refers to these as 'occasional poems', and notes her decision not to include them, though she gives no real reason.) It is clear that this book is primarily intended to be a relaxed, nostalgic ramble back through all those poems the reader already knows and loves.

Perhaps a little too relaxed, however. In spite of Lochhead's assertion in that she was 'interested in making … new connections' when it came to the ordering of the pieces, poems from the same collections are clumped together, sometimes in a very similar order to that in which they originally appeared. 'The Hickie', 'The Other Woman', 'Last Supper' and 'Everybody's Mother' are placed alongside one another in both *The Grimm Sisters* and this *Selected*. Three of the four poems from *Bagpipe Musak* are also included practically next to one another. This means that along with the nostalgia, there is also a feeling of dull repetition – not only have we seen all these poems before, we've seen them before exactly like this. This *Selected* provided a potential challenge: to surprise the reader into seeing these cherished poems with fresh eyes. This could have been achieved by interspersing them among their lesser-known cousins; by deliberately creating unusual juxtapositions on the page. Instead, the ordering of the poems seems all-too-obvious. Even when poems from different collections appear alongside one another, they are often grouped according to theme. *Memo for Spring*'s 'Revelation' and 'An Abortion' from *Dreaming Frankenstein*, for example: both poems use the farmyard setting to explore ideas about human sexuality and gender.

There are other odd editorial decisions, too. In several places, Lochhead has chosen poems that originally appeared in three parts, and in each case, she has selected only two of those parts for inclusion. The Spinster and the Bawd from *The Grimm Sisters*' 'The Furies' appear without the Harridan. *Dreaming Frankenstein* provides 'In the Dreamschool' and 'The Teachers', but not the third part, 'The Prize'. Perhaps most oddly, we do not get to hear 'What The Creature Said': the second, connecting part of the famous Frankenstein trio. Lochhead claims she did not want to over-think her selection – indeed, at one point she refers to it as 'a random flinging-together without much rhyme or reason' – and the reader is clearly not supposed to think too much about it either. However, it is difficult to prevent a sense of curiosity from developing when one notices these bizarre omissions.

But a volume of selected poems does have another purpose: it provides a starting point for those as yet unfamiliar with the writer's work to get a sense of exactly what it is they do. And apart from its almost total exclusion of the performance poetry side of her oeuvre, *A Choosing* is a pretty accurate representation of who Lochhead is as a poet. It can't be denied that her best and smartest lines do appear here. Lines like those at the end of 'Kidspoem/ Bairnsang', which illustrate the kind of literary scene into which Lochhead initially emerged – 'a very male landscape', says Carol Ann Duffy in her Introduction.

> [W]hen it came to writing it
> in black and white
> the way it had to be said
> was as if you were posh, grown-up, male, English and dead.

Also included are plenty of what Duffy refers to as 'monologues about ordinary women in trying or comic situations'. Poems like 'The Mirror's

Song', which explores the ridiculous and dangerously oppressive trappings of femininity.

> She'll crumple all the
> tracts and the adverts, shred
> all the wedding dresses, snap
> all the spike-heel icicles
> in the cave she will claw out of –
> a woman giving birth to herself.

And the absence of Lochhead's whip-smart, often slightly silly 'occasional poems' does heighten the poignancy of the 'paper poems' she has included. Many of the pieces here effectively mix bitter and sweet. For example, 'Poem for my Sister' juxtaposes the cosy image of the little girl's 'spindle-thin twelve-year-old legs' wobbling on high-heels with a stark warning about the emotional dangers of adulthood.

> I should not like to see her
> in my shoes.
> I wish she could stay
> sure-footed,
>   sensibly shod.

Even the seemingly careless 'flinging-together' of poems is a typical Lochhead statement. For her, poetry is supposed to be fun, accessible, and not too much like hard work. At the book's launch, she said, 'poets have a terrible habit of singing the song of themselves'. Perhaps she sees this slightly haphazard approach to a *Selected* as a way of railing against that. Indeed, one editorial decision in the book is clearly no accident: Lochhead leaves the reader to chew on the final poem, 'Poets Need Not'. A new piece, it sums up what she has learned from her many years in the poetry-writing business, and offers a cautionary tale for those looking to follow in her footsteps:

> This is a game
> you very seldom win
> and most of your efforts end up in the bin.

Claire Askew

The Roundabout Man. Sceptre. ISBN 9780340994320. PBK. £8.99
Clare Morrall

Is there really such a thing as a true story? Can you ever know whether an event you remember from childhood really happened, or you think you remember it because someone described it to you? The protagonist of Clare Morrall's fifth novel, *The Roundabout Man*, struggles with these very problems, magnified by the fact that his mother, a famous writer of Enid Blyton-esque children's stories, named her own protagonist after him. These stories, the Triplets and Quinn series, are so famous that no one can believe he's the real Quinn – particularly as he now lives in a caravan in the middle of a roundabout.

Quinn is an immensely likeable character, despite his flaws (which change depending on his age – neediness as a child, self-absorption as a twentysomething, elusiveness as an adult). We first meet him as a sixty-year-old man living a money-free existence in his caravan, scavenging for unfinished food in the service station cafeteria. Although this lifestyle might not suit everyone, it's the one Quinn has chosen – and he has a sense of humour about it. When a young journalist visits him, she asks what time it is.

> 'I listen to the sounds around me. 'About eight o'clock,' I say.
>
> I want her to ask how I can be so precise, so I can explain that I listen to nature, measure how far the sun has risen, recognise the call of the lark, the curlew, the wood pigeon, and assess the amount of moisture on the bark of the sycamores. But she doesn't ask. And, anyway, it wouldn't be true. 'You can tell from the traffic,' I say. 'It's the rush-hour.'

Despite the hints towards more serious issues such as domestic neglect and homelessness, *The Roundabout Man* is a charming, dreamy novel. There is the odd moment of unpleasantness – namely, Quinn being horribly beaten by a pair of youths – but in general the sadness is quiet, slow and whimsical: the yearning of a small boy for the affections of his distant mother and the father he never bothered to know. Perhaps the saddest sections are those dealing with Quinn's feelings at age twenty-one, after his father dies:

> It took me a while to work out that I missed him. I kept imagining he was still in his study, that he would emerge at suppertime, tall and slightly stooped, his glasses hovering dangerously on the end of his nose, and fix

me with his vaguely puzzled, amused look … I hadn't realised that he had been so present in my life. Was this grief?

And so we return to the novel's central concern: what is truth? What is reality? Quinn knows that his mother's rose-tinted stories do not represent his real childhood, but at times he doubts his own memories. It doesn't help that his triplet sisters all disagree over what really happened. Old-fashioned Fleur insists that everything in the books – including the finding of pirate treasure, the capturing of smugglers, and the discovery of a skeleton in a cupboard – all really happened, as unlikely as it may seem. Fashionable Zuleika takes the opposite stance, disdainfully claiming that not a single word of the stories is true. The third, Hetty, never expresses an opinion and distances herself entirely from the question.

Matters are complicated by Quinn's mother's Alzheimer's; when he visits her in her care home, she says 'Quinn doesn't really exist, you know … He was a character in one of my books.'

Dramatic tension is largely created by the reader's curiosity about how Quinn ended up living this life. It's unclear whether Quinn himself really knows. It may seem simplistic to explain away his lifestyle by drawing parallels with the childhood described in his mother's books, but at times the text leads us along that train of thought. Here is Quinn describing his caravan:

> The caravan is round and old-fashioned in design, a little shabby, nestling between the sycamores, but it looks cosy. A camp in the woods, a private place that adjusts to the rhythms of nature, enclosed by the ever-circling traffic.

It sounds like something from a cute children's book, and it's easy to imagine the fictional Quinn hiding out in just such a place.

Although there is a lot going on, the pace never feels rushed. Each location and phase of Quinn's life is vividly and lovingly drawn. It is perhaps unavoidable that a novel with such quirky elements will feel somewhat quaint, but Morrall tempers the twee perfectly with occasional dark moments, the power of Quinn's humour and moments of self-doubt. Quinn struggles with other people's ideas of what he should be, and at times it feels that abandonment of his previous life is the only solution for him. The truth always exists somewhere, though, and *The Roundabout Man* ends on an uplifting note: we do not need to be dragged down by our past after all.

Kirsty Logan

New Ways to Kill Your Mother: Writers and Their Families. Penguin Viking. ISBN 9780670918164. HBK. £20
Colm Tóibín

There are perhaps three main kinds of reader who would want to pick up a collection of largely review-based essays by a famous author. There is the fan or devoted scholar who will want in any case to have everything with their man's name on it with a view to assuaging their completist conscience and deepening their holistic engagement with his thought and sensibility. There is the reader more drawn to topics than particular authors, who will trust that the designated title will indeed prove the designing force behind the collection, and who will figure that since the author is widely admired he will have much of interest and benefit to say on the matter to hand. There is the more generically driven reader, rarer in the field of review essays and criticism than elsewhere, who will be seeking information, certainly, but who will also want to see how the job is done, what useful ways of doing this kind of work can be learned here (often, unavoidably, in the hope that the writers and books covered will in fact be so well *done* as to preclude the necessity of ever having to actually read them).

While in the case of *New Ways to Kill Your Mother* we might also want to tack on the reader immediately gratified by any sight of fine book-production standards, our three readers to hand will all find plenty to wonder at and about in Colm Tóibín's new essay collection, whether they indulge in the great joy of dipping that books like this provide for, or instead proceed sequentially from Tóibín's overture on Jane Austen and Henry James through his two parts of seven essays each, respectively titled, no-nonsensewise, 'Ireland' and 'Elsewhere'.

Tóibín's most notable statement of his governing position on literature comes early on in the Austen and James essay, in a paragraph that so perfectly puts the case for what might be called a humane formalism, so concisely encapsulates an entire aesthetic, that it can already be heard slotting as a block-quote into rightful pride of place in the introductions to every thesis and dissertation on him over the next good while. Tóibín does not insist that 'character in fiction is merely a verbal construct and bears no relation to the known world', but neither will he have any dealings with simplistic moral criticism that fumbles the relation between word and world at the expense of what's actually involved in the act of creation: 'A novel is a set of strategies, closer to something in mathematics or quantum physics than something in ethics or sociology. It is a release of certain energies and a dramatisation of how these energies might be controlled, given shape.' The reader intent on garnering Tóibín's reading principles has to depend on smaller moments thereafter, though the ensuing essays are evidence in practice of his thinking about literature as a made phenomenon, the relation of which to the world is paralleled by the various confidence tricks those doing the making devise to mould themselves. In all the essays, there is nothing fallacious about the biographical approach; while keeping his writers' writing to the fore, Tóibín is vitally interested in the ways particular lives inflect, and are in turn inflected by, acts of composition. Biographies, autobiographies and collections of letters are the regular premises for the pieces in the first place.

In a review of R.F. Foster's *Paddy and Mr Punch* for the *LRB* in November 1993, itself titled 'New Ways of Killing Your Father', Tóibín spoke of the early need he had felt in the face of an imposed sense of Irish history for 'a most subversive idea, a new way of killing your father, starting from scratch, creating a new self'. It would be conventional enough at this stage to ascribe this imperative towards contradistinctive self-creation to either Tóibín's revisionist convictions or to his situation as a gay writer emerging in an unamenable time and place. But, while there is therefore a clear enough organic relation between Tóibín's own biography and his preoccupation here with forms of creation and self-creation, he makes it clear that there is much more at stake than any easy autobiographical transference. So entirely does he usually keep his own personality out of the critical equation, so wary is he of taking any easily identifiable moral position, that those who want Tóibín himself to always come clearly to the surface are likely to be disappointed. The personal, and occasionally the social or national contexts (as with Brian Moore, Sebastian Barry, Borges), in which the creativity of others was fostered or hassled, and crucial individual works that emerged thereby, are primary. Creative sensibilities, practically by definition, almost always have to make their own room for themselves, in their own time and place, within and without their own families. The house of fiction is often as not built by way of testing or shaking, estranging into the distance, virtually destroying outright, the home once known. Synge and Beckett and their mothers; the Yeats brothers and the James brothers and their respective fathers; the contrasting moods in the ways Roddy Doyle and Hugo Hamilton have written about their parents; the deeply touching relationship between Tennessee Williams and his sister Rose; the amazing tight ball of contradictions that was John Cheever: all of these, topped by the intriguing psychiatric performance that was Thomas Mann's family, provide rich material for Tóibín's examination of the 'stealth' and 'deceit' writers must necessarily nurture to allow their fictions evolve from the energy-sapping embrace of close human relationships. And it is one of his feats that he explores the whole possibility that 'A happy childhood may make good citizens, but it is not a help for those of us facing a blank page' without a trace of the psychobabble one might usually expect from such a topic.

Even when his earlier work in journalism gave way to the career in fiction for which he is now attended, Tóibín remained a ubiquitous commentator and critic, and he has especially continued to add his voice to cultural debate through reviewing for the major organs both sides of the Atlantic. Since reviewing continues to be seen in many professional literary quarters as irreversibly *mere* journalism, some will therefore see it as regrettable that he didn't do more patent procedural justice here to the practice as a critical genre. It is not that essays such as this shouldn't be packaged and titled in a new way (the volume, after all, is a selection in that Tóibín has chosen which of his many reviews and other pieces to include under his rubric, which to exclude). Nor is it that such collections need necessarily be emphatic about their origins (as in, for instance, Christopher Ricks' *Reviewery*, or Updike's perennial subtitle of *Essays and Criticism*). It is rather that there seems no real reason to not help readers immediately identify the origin of a review essay on the page itself, even if not pinning a piece immediately to its source does allow scope for changes to the original text. There are discreet ways of providing information on sources and the book under review (Christopher Hitchens' *Arguably* is a recent example), and there is surely no need for a publisher to worry that the provision of such basic information in a header or footer would prove dissuasive since any reader already drawn to read a book of criticism is unlikely to blanch that easily. Because of the strategy of presentation here, where the titles under review are all retained for a Bibliography at the end and where the sources of the individual pieces are given, incompletely, in the Acknowledgements, the reader can sometimes feel unsure within individual essays about which book is the principal point of reference for quotes or the discussion generally.

The point is that Tóibín is a highly readable book critic, from whom a distinct style of reviewing can be learned, and who should maybe therefore be seen to fly this generic flag when he can. Along with liberal paraphrase, his typical reviewing strategy is to allow his subjects a firm hold of their own rope, quoting them regularly and sometimes at length. And, to encourage independent reading, this is almost always done with no advance instruction from him through verb or adverb by way of narrowing the possible implications of his chosen quotes: 'he wrote', or close version thereof, is his standard set-up. Because of the variety of objectivity Tóibín practises in this way; because he communicates a buoyant curiosity about the humdrum actualities of people's internal and external lives while also concentrating on what's written on writers' actual pages; because his sheer enthusiasm demands the expansion of horizons (this reviewer will be giving James Baldwin a proper go after the two essays on him here); because he allies plain speaking to fluency; because he holds to words such as *genius, beauty, exquisite* – this, together, is why we should have such essay-driven collections as *New Ways to Kill Your Mother* on our 'critical practice' courses in our universities instead of books theoretically over-determined and deadened by moral posturing. More downright entertainment would be had, what's more.

John Kenny

The Salt Harvest. Seren. ISBN 9781854115492. PBK. £8.99
Eoghan Walls

Eoghan Walls's first collection announces him as a poet firmly pitched against abstraction, and one in whose work topical reference jostles with the longer view – both back into the past and forward into the future. If this makes him sound like Heaney, it shouldn't: though born and raised in Derry, Walls wields a voice which strikes out on its own and, like all the best poetic voices, seems almost entirely to lack antecedents. Occasionally there are hints of Muldoon, and Heaney is sparred with in the brilliant 'Thirteen Foot by Six', which delineates a yard where 'no kittens [are] drowned in the coal bucket' and 'Blackberries are banned, / as is frogspawn'. But in style, outlook and subject Walls is his own man: here, 'praise be', is a voice bringing something really new, and without straining the buttons to achieve it.

Novelty for its own sake is not an unquestionable good, but the poems of *The Salt Harvest* don't 'do' new in the effortful fashion of cladding themselves in edgy garb or throwing up the head at formal convention. Rather, what we witness here is the emergence of a distinctive sensibility, and the (highly unusual) admission into poems of the whole being behind their creation.

In the title poem, Walls counsels himself to 'Evaporate the sludge for the residue', but one of the best things about his work is its refusal to tolerate such quality distinctions. 'Hole' (as in 'anus') rhymes with 'soul' in 'A Bird in the Hand'; mentos and coke unite to form 'mentos bombs' and, startlingly, parallel a soul pausing 'on its long trek in the moondust' in 'Small Explosions'. The sinister Ulster Scots voice in 'Lega' Ten'er', a poem with a sharp political edge, is impishly force-fed lines such as 'yir wan in the Shanty Mobile refuse ye a single Benson' – whimsy and *joie-de-vivre* in language (a 'language', one might add, not beloved of the Derry Catholic) carry this poem forward equally with its darker message of abusive power. 'Pissabed' describes dandelions as flowers that root both 'where dogs have pissed and in the holy garden', and this is a fitting emblem for the poems themselves, which offer strange, but strangely perfect, conjunctions.

The notion of interface and bizarre transition animates the deeps of the poems as well as their surface details, and is in fact at the heart of the book. First collections are many-faceted; however, Walls is a precision organiser, and this is not a first book without a clear trajectory, even if the path leads to progressive confusion. From early poems in which folk remedies and religion are invoked for succour and guidance, and 'signs' such as the 'downturned face' of the Virgin 'off the Meath coast' are read as having import and intent, the collection progresses into less reassuring territory. 'The Naming of the Rat', where Christ reveals to the rodent its unpalatable destiny, is met later by the 'negative baptism' of 'Taking Names', where the sea 'eats the damp names of children' and 'The sign has been clipped, / neatly torn by the Bradleys … // Or maybe the Keaveneys' (itself a neat revision of Patrick Kavanagh's 'Epic', in which the invocation of family names in small town life confirms, rather than erases, set coordinates). The face of the Virgin in 'Star of the Sea' morphs, first, into the scientifically detailed immaculate conception of a shark, which is equally miraculous but portends nothing ('Lights above the water / were only torches held by men from the aquarium'), and, second, into the motile and unnerving 'face of a girl' who represents, in the science fiction setting of 'The Martians', the crux between humanity and a post-human planet:

> The bedsheets are sodden
>
> with blood and your wife
>
> has stopped calling for God.
>
> This is the new life
>
> forcing its slick curls
>
> part mucous, part light,
>
> through a gap between worlds

Similarly, where poems early in the book explore our physical tyranny over nature (man literally consumes-to-contain everything, from cockles to mercury, and what he doesn't scoff he pulls the innards out of), later poems like 'The Long Horizon' and 'Hibernation of the Canals' have the natural (and galactic) worlds bite back, driving the human into fragile vulnerability. Sure physical presence shifts to the panicked tracing of 'prints', and 'weighty creatures' give way to flimsy ones – 'somebody's dachshund that shudders turds inside a tyre'.

These transitions are not handled bluntly, but with subtlety and care: worlds are interwoven with one another, and the balance shifts continually, almost beyond notice. Walls is a master *par excellence* of traditional forms (as well as a highly impressive inventor of new ones), and especially favours *terza rima* which, along with the pantoum, offers the perfect vehicle for his interlinking of and nuanced shifting between things. Again, formal deployment works in accordance with the book's overall development: whereas, in 'Myrrh', *terza rima* allows for the synchronicity of past and present, end-stopped stanzas mirroring controlled progression, 'Vertigo on the Glenshane Pass' is a single sentence which, like the action described, tumbles 'in perpetual freefall'. 'A Boiled Egg' ties itself into self-defeating (and self-eating) circularity by having the last rhyme hark back to the first, and – wait for it – 'The Martians' is written in backwards *terza rima*. This last may be more an example of Walls's fun-loving instinct than his yen for serious statement, but that shouldn't stand against it. You needn't be po-faced to be a serious poet, whatever the phonetics of the word suggest.

Miriam Gamble

Bring Me the Head of Ryan Giggs. Tindal Street Press. ISBN 9781906994389.
PBK. £12.99
Rodge Glass

At what point, one wonders, did the English Premiership jump the reality shark?

Could it have been when Paul Gascoigne approached the besieged Raoul Moult, offering fishing lines and a takeaway meal? Or when the winger, Nani, commissioned a lifesize bronze statue of himself for display in his living room? Or was it the second Joey Barton began tweeting epigrams from Nietzsche?

The novelist prepared to take on this world has a decision to make. The temptation – the imperative, actually – is to construct an aesthetic half way between *Caligula* and *OK Magazine* that reflects the insane pitch of the modern game. But then, do that and you're suddenly writing *Footballers' Wives*.

Rodge Glass sidesteps these concerns by rewinding two decades; locating his story during English football's Jurassic Age: the early nineties. A period when players only crossed into civilian life after the onset of bankruptcy or to explain the benefits of drinking semi-skimmed milk. When football brightened up weekends and the odd Wednesday. When it was recognisably earthbound.

Ryan Giggs occupies a unique position in the middle of all this. The last twelve months may have shown Giggs to be au fait with the workings of a super-injunction, but prior to that, as the last survivor of the old First Division days, he had become an emblem of a dead era: a kind of High Def Harry Patch.

Mikey Wilson earns the nickname Little Giggs while slaloming through the ranks of Man Utd youth. The actual Giggs, of course, is always a step or two ahead, but so long as Mikey's progress seems destined to end as a first-team regular it hardly counts as a problem. That's until the day of his Old Trafford debut when, while chasing a pass from Giggs, Mikey suffers an injury that finishes his career.

Two decades later and he's still turning up at Old Trafford – manically attempting to start singalongs amongst 'the prawn sandwich brigade', reminding people who he 'used to be', and cultivating an obsession with his gilded former teammate: an obsession that manifests itself in vivid, fetishised dreams, and trolling binges on United-based websites. He has also taken to writing letters to David Beckham, offering his services as a babysitter.

Glass's novel finds the old footballing world collide with the new. And much like the infamous Roy Keane 'tackle' on Alf Inge Haaland, the old world gets carried off semi-conscious on a stretcher, its assailant standing over it, muttering insults.

Using Playercam, Mikey's maniacal focus on Giggs bears an unmistakable similarity to *The King of Comedy*'s deluded Rubert Pupkin. In wide shot, however, it's a story of human detritus and second-hand rage. Glass writes with real romance about the burgeoning and blooding of young footballing talent, but as the story develops, and Mikey locks into a life of bitterness and poverty, the narrative brims with cynicism and fury.

There's a darkness at the heart of the English Football pantomime, Glass contends – one that encourages festering resentment and troubled psyches. Bitterness and fury, it seems, are the real seagulls following the Premiership trawler.

Colin Carberry

A Time of Tyrants: Scotland and the Second World War. Birlinn. ISBN 9781843410553 HBK. £25
Trevor Royle

Trevor Royle gave readers of the Scottish literary magazine *Fras* a fascinating glimpse recently of what was to become one of the major strands of *A Time of Tyrants*. The book is an all-encompassing study of the socio-economic, political and artistic implications of the Second World War in Scotland and the ways in which Scotland contributed to resolutions of this global conflict. This is very much the follow-on from his objectively similar study of Scotland during the First World War, entitled *Flowers of the Forest*. To return to *Fras*, Royle published a digest of some of the notable wartime poetry and novels written by Scots either at home or in action. Under the title 'Keep Listening for Reveille' it alludes to a phrase from Hamish Henderson's 'Ninth Elegy' of his war-time poem sequence *Elegies for the Dead in Cyrenaica*. While this is a significant and under-researched area, critical treatments of poets like Henderson, who fought in offensives in the Maghreb Conflict, have already occupied essay length studies by both Roderick Watson and Angus Calder. In many ways *A Time of Tyrants* reads like precisely the type of even-handed and thorough-going study that would have been keenly read by Angus Calder, if not written by him.

Royle's study is framed in literary terms but is far from simply literary précis or criticism. The title *A Time of Tyrants* is drawn from a poem by William Soutar, which promises light from 'the darkest loam' and the 'catacomb'. Although Soutar died in 1943, he is often thought of as the ghostly father-figure of the second wave of the Scottish Literary Renaissance. Much of his work from the thirties is highly prescient in terms of the Second World War. Royle's task, however, is not to simply look at literature as the only gauge of the times but instead he sets out to prove his claim that the Second World War was like no other in that it was a democratic conflict where no one was unaffected, even in the remotest Highlands and islands. Royle uses first-hand oral and written accounts to bring his points to life and shows how social boundaries were profoundly mixed up during the war: creating both tension, racial and ideological, but also scope for new interactions and relationships.

Whenever a poet or writer is mentioned, such as Hugh MacDiarmid's gruelling lot as a lathe-turner on the Clyde, Royle expands his scope from the minutiae of day-to-day life. He reconnects with events of grave importance on battlefields or in politics so that the study is never static and weaves together various cultural and military strands. Unsurprisingly, depictions of conflict involving Scottish regiments abound, but Royle's meticulous eye for detail and research make sure that events become animated without being in any way sensationalist. That said, there are passages that startle the reader – such as a compelling account of Scotland's failed foray into bio-chemical warfare, testing an anthrax bomb on sheep on Gruinard Island. Royle thus shows us the extremes people were forced to go to because of the war.

The layout of the chapters is done so well that the reader experiences something of the trajectory of the war from both a home-front and combatant perspective. The book opens with an air of merriment brought on by the preparations for the 1938 Empire Exhibition in Bellahouston Park which Royle describes as a great futuristic 'last hurrah' before Scotland and the rest of the world is plunged into global warfare. The chapters that follow deal firstly with the announcement of war, then the lull in hostilities described as the 'phoney war', before moving on to catalogue the disasters and hardships of the war.

In Chapter 8 the crucial turning point is reached where 'the balance of the war falls in favour of the Allies'. From then on the book moves towards victory by either digging or fighting so that in the closing chapter celebrations are once again being planned for VE Day, avoiding the mass inebriation in the streets that followed the armistice at the end of the First World War. Although Royle captures, as Soutar's poem does, a sense of a brighter future, it is nonetheless one that is more sober, and tinged with loss. Royle's epilogue discusses the decline in Nationalist fervour because of the exigent need for collaboration and solidarity during the war, to its eventual and what John Herdman describes as 'furtive' resurgence in the sixties, moving towards the opening of the Scottish Parliament in 1999. Royle expresses a muted optimism for an independent Scotland as one of the great trophies of peace fought for nearly sixty years ago in the Second World War.

With its democratic approach of focusing equally on the home front and fighting populace (Scottish peers sometimes emerging in a less favourable light than Axis POWs) *A Time of Tyrants* is gripping in its detail as in its inclusivity. Consistently readable and informative, it will resonate with readers of whatever level of engagement with the history of the Second World War in Scotland.

Richie McCaffery

Notes on Contributors

Fred D'Aguiar was born in London in 1960 of Guyanese parents and brought up in Guyana. His *New and Selected, An English Sampler*, was published by Chatto in 2001 and *Continental Shelf* (Carcanet, 2009) was a Poetry Book Society Choice and shortlisted for the T.S. Eliot Prize 2009.

Claire Askew's poetry has appeared in a variety of publications including the *Guardian* and *Poetry Scotland*, and most recently in *PANK* and *Dark Horse*. Her debut pamphlet collection, *The Mermaid and the Sailors* (2011), was shortlisted for the Eric Gregory Award. A poem from the collection also won the 2010 Virginia Warbey Poetry Prize. Claire is reading for a PhD in Creative Writing from the University of Edinburgh, and works as a lecturer in Literature and Communication at Edinburgh's Telford College.

Ciaran Berry's first book, *The Sphere of Birds*, was published by the Gallery Press in 2008 and was awarded the Jerwood Aldeburgh First Collection Prize and the Michael Murphy Memorial Prize. He's working on a second collection called *The Dead Zoo*.

Marianne Boruch's work includes seven poetry collections, most recently *The Book of Hours*, two books of essays, and a memoir, *The Glimpse Traveler*. She teaches at Purdue University (US), and is currently a Fulbright/Visiting Professor at the University of Edinburgh.

Ron Butlin was recently re-appointed as Edinburgh Makar. His novel *The Sound of My Voice* was included in the *Guardian*'s 1,000 Books Everyone Must Read. His new collection of poetry, *The Magicians of Edinburgh*, will be published in August. Ron lives in Edinburgh with his wife, the writer Regi Claire. www.ronbutlin.co.uk

Ian Campbell retired in 2009 from the English Department at the University of Edinburgh, where he is Emeritus Professor of Scottish and Victorian Literature, and teaching fellow. He has worked since 1964 on *The Collected Letters of Thomas and Jane Welsh Carlyle*, of which he is now one of the senior editors, and has published widely on Victorian and Scottish topics.

Colin Carberry lives and works in Belfast. He is the co-writer of *Good Vibrations,* the upcoming biopic of Terri Hooley, Belfast's 'Godfather of Punk'.

Charles Doersch is a poet living in the Rocky Mountains where he teaches writing at the University of Colorado. His recent poetry has appeared in the *New Criterion*, *Academic Questions* and the *Hudson Review*.

Sarah Dunnigan works in the English Literature Department at Edinburgh University. She has written about medieval and Renaissance Scottish literature, ballads, Burns and contemporary women writers. She has recently edited Violet Jacob's *The Golden Heart* and is completing a book about the imaginative life of fairies from the medieval to Romantic periods in Scotland.

Colin Graham is co-editor of *The Irish Review*. He writes for *Source* photography magazine and for *The Vacuum*. His books include *Deconstructing Ireland* and *Ideologies of Epic*. He teaches at NUI Maynooth.

Miriam Gamble lectures in creative writing by online learning at the University of Edinburgh. Her first collection of poems, *The Squirrels are Dead*, is published by Bloodaxe and won a Somerset Maugham Award in 2011.

Jen Hadfield has published two collections of poetry with Bloodaxe Books. Her second, *Nigh-No-Place,* was shortlisted for the Forward Prize in 2007 and won the T.S. Eliot Prize for poetry in 2008. She lives in Shetland, where she is currently the Shetland Library's Reader-in-Residence. She blogs intermittently at rogueseeds. blogspot.com.

Doug Johnstone is a writer, journalist and musician. He's had four novels published, most recently *Hit & Run* (Faber). Doug regularly writes for various newspapers and magazines, and until recently he was Writer in Residence at the University of Strathclyde.

Maria Johnston was born in Dublin. She holds a PhD in English from Trinity College Dublin and has taught poetry and literature at Mater Dei Institute (DCU), Trinity College Dublin and Christ Church, Oxford. She frequently contributes essays on and reviews of contemporary poetry to journals such as *Poetry Ireland Review* and *Tower Poetry* and is the co-editor (with Philip Coleman) of *Reading Pearse Hutchinson: 'From Findrum to Fisterra'* (Irish Academic Press, 2011).

John Kenny is John McGahern Lecturer in Creative Writing at NUI Galway where he is Director of the BA with Creative Writing, Acting Director of the MA in Journalism and Academic Director of The International John McGahern Seminar. He is author of *John Banville* (2009) and editor of *The John McGahern Yearbook* (4 vols.).

Katherine Leyton is a poet from Toronto, Canada. Her work has appeared in a number of Canadian literary journals, including *Room* and the *Malahat Review*. She is also the founder of HowPedestrian.ca, a highly unorthodox video poetry blog.

Kirsty Logan lives in Glasgow. She recently completed her first novel, *Rust and Stardust*, and a short story collection, *The Rental Heart and Other Fairytales*. Her work has been published in over eighty anthologies and literary magazines, and broadcast on BBC Radio 4. kirstylogan.com

Martin MacInnes lives in Edinburgh. He is completing a book about fiction, biography and evolution, called *Transcription*. 'Ascension Island' is an extract from a chapter.

Richie McCaffery is a Carenegie Research Scholar at the University of Glasgow, researching the Scottish poets of World War Two towards a PhD in Scottish Literature. His first collection, *Spinning Plates*, has just been published by Happenstance Press.

Tony McKibbin teaches adult education classes at the University of Edinburgh, mainly on film. He writes for a number of journals and magazines, including *Senses of Cinema* and *Film International*.

Willy Maley is Professor of English Literature at Glasgow University. In 1995 he co-founded with Philip Hobsbaum the Creative Writing programme there. His recent work includes *Muriel Spark for Starters* (Capercaillie, 2008), and, as co-editor with Michael Gardiner, *The Edinburgh Companion to Muriel Spark* (Edinburgh University Press, 2010).

Sean O'Brien's seventh collection, *November* (Picador), was shortlisted for the Griffin International Poetry Prize. His *Collected Poems* is to appear in December 2012. He is Professor of Creative Writing at Newcastle University.

Yasmin Sulaiman is a freelance writer, and a University of Edinburgh English Literature graduate. She writes about contemporary books and theatre in Scotland and London, and is a previous winner of the Allan Wright Award at the Edinburgh Festival Fringe.

Alice Thompson has been writer in residence for Shetland and novelist in residence for St Andrews University. She is a Lecturer in Creative Writing at Edinburgh University. In 1996 she was joint winner (with Graham Swift) of the James Tait Black Memorial Prize for her first novel, *Justine*, and has since published *Pandora's Box*, *Pharos*, *The Falconer* and *The Existential Detective*.

Marina Tsvetaeva was described by Brodsky as the most significant phenomenon in Russian poetry since Pushkin. She emigrated in 1922 and lived near Prague, then Paris, returning to the Soviet Union in 1939, where she took her own life in 1941. Her letters and notebooks are gradually taking their place alongside her poetry as an achievement without parallel in early twentieth century European literature.

Christopher Whyte's fifth collection of poems in Gaelic, *An Daolag Shìonach*, is due out later this year. A volume of some 170 Tsvetaeva translations, *Moscow in the Plague Year*, will be published by Archipelago Books of New York in 2013. Christopher Whyte lives between Budapest and Slovenia but will be resident in Glasgow again from next September.

Allan Wilson is from Glasgow. His short story collection, *Wasted in Love*, was published by Cargo in October 2011 and has been shortlisted for the Scottish Book of the Year Award 2012. He is working on his first novel, *Meat*.

Li San Xing's poetry and prose has appeared in *The Rialto*, *Smiths Knoll*, *The Liberal*, *Gutter* and *Short FICTION*. He was shortlisted for an Eric Gregory Award in 2010. He was born in Edinburgh and lives in London.

How to Subscribe to Edinburgh Review

Individual subscriptions (3 issues annually) £20 within the UK; £28 abroad.

Institutional subscriptions (3 issues annually) £35 within the UK; £43 abroad.

You can subscribe online at www.edinburgh-review.com
or send a cheque to

Edinburgh Review
22a Buccleuch Place
Edinburgh EH8 9LN

Most back issues are available at £7.99 each.

You'll find the new *Edinburgh Review* website at

http://www.edinburgh-review.com

Please join us on Facebook and Twitter.